The Ghosts of Cawood Castle

A Novel

Chris Cawood

Magnolia Hill Press, Knoxville, Tennessee, USA

A work of fiction with historical references

Printed in the United States by KDP

Cover Design by Getcovers.com

Library of Congress Control Number: 2023911118

Contents

Introduction

When American author and lawyer Chris Cawood goes looking for his family history in his ancestral Village of Cawood in North Yorkshire, he uncovers more than his genealogy research had shown.

He had traced his Cawood line back twenty-two generations to 1200 and Johannes De Cawood of the village by the same name. Having found his ten generations of Cawoods in America, he was anxious to see what lay ahead in the village.

Cawood Castle had been mainly destroyed after the English Civil War, but the stone gatehouse remained as a sentry in the middle of the village. He had rented the three-story structure for a week. Although the basic part was about six hundred years old, bathrooms, a kitchen, and electricity had been added. It was going to be a fabulous holiday for him, his wife, Sara, and two granddaughters, Katie, 16, and Ashlynn, 13.

Visits to Selby Abbey, where his ancestor, David Cawood, was abbot from 1263 to 1270, and to York Minster heightened his curiosity.

But the first night at the castle gatehouse propelled him to meet the Ghosts of Cawood Castle. A spirit whose name was Servant was the first to appear. He had lived at the castle in the 1400s and early 1500s. Servant proved invaluable in being able to bring the other spirits who had once lived or visited the castle for meetings at the gatehouse.

Four English kings, a queen, and ten archbishops of York appear and tell of their lives and experiences at the castle.

Finally, King Henry VIII comes to be tried. The Jury has nine archbishops and three kings. The prosecutor is Cardinal Thomas Wolsey. Queen Catherine Howard and Thomas Culpeper are witnesses.

The verdict?

Chapter One

The Train Ride

Trains in England run on time and fast when they are not on strike.

My wife, Sara, two of our granddaughters, Katie, 16, and Ashlynn, 13, and I walked through the King's Cross Station in London to board the 9:30 a.m. train to Selby.

It was about one hundred seventy-five miles from London, going north to Selby. Then it would be another five miles by bus from Selby to my ancestral village of Cawood on the River Ouse in North Yorkshire.

In my quest for my Cawood ancestors, I had studied what was written about Selby, Cawood, and York, which formed a triangle of a few miles on each side. I was particularly interested in the remains of Cawood Castle in the village of Cawood.

The remains of the castle were now owned by Landmark Trust, who made it available for rental. All that remained was the three-story gatehouse and what was known as the Banqueting Hall, although it probably had been used more for stables for horses and storage. The second and third floors of the Gatehouse had been modeled into two large rooms with beds and a small kitchen. Two bathrooms were accessible from a narrow spiral stone staircase. We had booked a week's holiday.

We had stayed three days in London at The House of Toby, a pub that had been converted into a small hotel. It was just a half-mile's walk from there to the beautiful King's Cross and St. Pancras stations.

We had ridden the double-decker tour buses and seen many interesting sights. A riverboat ride on the Thames and a visit to the Royal Mews were two of the granddaughters' favorites. The royal horses and carriages at the Royal Mews brought sparkling eyes to my granddaughters. They were amazed.

I visited St. Paul's Cathedral, where my grandfather, fifteen generations back, is buried. John Cawood, who died in 1572, was a Royal Printer for Queen Mary and Queen Elizabeth I. John was born in the Village of Cawood, where we were off to visit. John's exact burial site is lost to history as the original St. Paul's Cathedral burned in the Great London Fire of 1666. But his earthly remains lie there somewhere, and I must have walked over them. John was also one of the founders of the Stationers Guild. I took a tour of Stationers Hall which is near St. Paul's and which John had helped with its beginnings.

Our train's departure was announced, and we trudged toward the loading platform with each of us rolling a large suitcase. A nice young couple helped us lift our items of luggage onto the train and place them in the storage compartments. We found our seats and settled in for a nearly two-hour ride to Selby. The girls were immediately on their phones and other electronic devices while Sara and I sat back to enjoy the view and take some time off from walking.

There was just a slight jog as the train pulled out and gathered some speed. The industrial part of London and high rises passed on both sides. This was not the touristy side of the city.

Soon, the industrial areas gave way to residential areas with green grass. It was early May, and flowers were beginning to grow and blossom. Within a half hour, we were passing farms where sheep grazed. The train was now charging along between a hundred and one hundred twenty-five miles per hour, but I couldn't tell it as the ride was rather smooth.

I sat back and retrieved my thick notebook, where I had written down some of my research on my Cawood ancestors and the towns we were going to visit.

According to my study, I was the twenty-second generation removed from John de Cawood of the 1200s. I was among the tenth generation of Cawoods in America. Stephen Cawood had sailed to Charles County, Maryland, around 1667 as an indentured servant to Lord Baltimore's son. Coming with him, also as indentured servants, were his future wife and another couple of friends who would also later marry.

From Port Tobacco, Maryland, Stephen had done well upon his discharge from being indentured. He came into possession of six hundred acres which he named Hull Plantation. Port Tobacco, as its name implies, was an export location for tobacco to go to England. Once the county seat of Charles County, it now only has a population of twenty-five. Sediment has covered what was a deep-water port to where now it can only be used for recreational boats.

Unfortunately, Stephen was killed a few years later in what was then known as an Indian war. His grave is unknown but is believed to be across the river in Maryland from where George Washington later built Mount Vernon in Virginia. Stephen fathered a child, another Stephen, who carried on the Cawood DNA.

From Maryland, the Cawoods migrated to Virginia, Kentucky, Ohio, Tennessee, and nearly every other state.

Two years before my trip to London, my brother and I had taken what we termed the Cawood Heritage Tour to visit places the Cawoods lived in Tennessee, Virginia, and Maryland. We were able to identify the Cawood farm in Speedwell (Claiborne County), Tennessee, from the early 1800s and where our ancestors lived in the 1780s near Glade Springs and Saltville, Virginia.

We drove around Charles County, Maryland, but were unable to locate precisely what had been the Hull Plantation of our original Stephen Cawood of the 1670s. We had probably driven by the plantation, which I knew was located near Mattawoman Creek. We crossed the creek several times without finding Stephen's farm.

From that trip tracing and chasing my ancestors and their homes, I determined to go to England and try to find out why Stephen had left England to come to America. What had he left behind?

I had seen on the map of Yorkshire a town named Kingston Upon Hull and wondered if that was where Stephen had found the name for his plantation—Hull. Maybe it was with fond memories he thought of the Kingston Upon Hull in England, which was just thirty or forty miles from Cawood in Yorkshire.

More farms with new fields plowed and planted and sheep grazing nearby passed in my view out the train's windows. Gazing down at my notes and research, I counted six Stephen Cawoods and nine John Cawoods in my ancestral line. I had the years of their births and the dates of their deaths in my notes. Their life spans were fairly normal--most around sixty years. My Great Grandfather, Stephen Harrison Cawood, was the longest-lived—from 1841 to 1936.

The first Cawood of record was John (Johannes) De Cawood. From the records I had, he lived from around 1200 to 1260. His son, David Cawood, made it to seventy-five (1240-1315). He served as Abbott of Selby Abbey from 1263 to 1270.

I shook my head and ran my thumb through the pages of research. I was going to visit an area where my ancestors lived eight hundred years ago. I looked out the window and tried to imagine what this area looked like eight hundred years before. My ancestors, two hundred years before 1200, were the keepers of the King's forests in part of Yorkshire. But my view of this area showed very few, if any, trees.

When I turned back to my pages of research, I noticed at one time I had written the numbers down of how many "grandfathers" I would have had going back twenty-two generations. I had two grandfathers, four great-grandfathers, eight great-great grandfathers and on and on—doubling every generation.

Theoretically, nine generations back when Stephen came to America, I could have had two hundred fifty-six "grandfathers." I say "theoretically," because there was bound to be some overlap of marriages and such in that period of time. And going back twenty-two generations, I could have had over two million different "grandfathers" and the same number of "grandmothers." The family tree certainly would have spread out into many branches, twigs, leaves—and perhaps a few nuts.

Yet, I was following and chasing only one line—the Cawood line. I was going straight back through every "grandfather" whose surname was Cawood. I knew I had Trotters, Jones, Rogers, Walkers, and many other heritage lines in my ancestry. But my focus had been strictly on the Cawood line going back twenty-two generations to the Village of Cawood in North Yorkshire that lay on the River Ouse.

What I was researching would have been anathema to many "true" genealogists, since I was only following one line of my ancestry. "Cawood" was certainly a more easily researched name than Smith, Jones, or some other common name. Although there were now several thousand Cawoods in the United States, more than ninety percent of them are descendants of the original Stephen Cawood who came to America around 1667.

When I sent my DNA to the Ancestry site, they returned my results a short time later. My DNA heritage was sixty-six percent from what is now England and twenty-two percent from Scotland. I looked at the map of the United Kingdom and saw that North Yorkshire and Scotland were not all that far apart.

The train slowed and stopped at Doncaster. We didn't have to change trains. I stood and stretched. The granddaughters glanced up.

"Is this where we get off?" Katie asked.

"No. Another quarter hour or so," I said.

Their eyes returned to their phones and the games they were playing. Sara was listening to an audiobook through her phone and earbuds.

There were a few people getting off the train at this stop and some more getting on. Within five minutes, we were on the way again.

There is something about a train ride that is so relaxing. I placed my notebook on the seat beside me and closed my eyes. Like a babe in a cradle, the gentle rolling of the train put me to napping.

I was awakened from my short nap by the announcement that Selby was our next stop. I told my granddaughters and Sara to prepare to get off. We had to move swiftly to retrieve our luggage and prepare to disembark. The train's schedule waits for no one.

The Selby station was barely populated when we got off. We stood on the platform, wondering how to get to the street. Then I noticed the stairway that would take us up to another landing to walk above the railroad tracks. On the far side was the ticket office and waiting area. Up the twenty steps pulling our luggage across the walkway, and then down the twenty steps, finally reaching the exit to the street.

I had checked what transport was available from Selby the approximately five miles to the Cawood Castle Gatehouse. The best way, it seemed to me, was to take the 42 Bus from the Selby bus station. It had a stop immediately in front of the Castle Gatehouse on its route to York. To get to the bus station to board the 42, we had to walk about a half mile down a gently sloping sidewalk toward Selby Abbey.

A stop at Selby Abbey would be a welcome break in the walk to the bus. It was a magnificent building. We could tour the grand old church parts of which dated from William the Conqueror. The building and Abbey had seen many periods of flourishing and decline from 1100 to present. Decay, part of the building falling, and the great fire of 1908 were some of the problems the abbots and leaders of the church faced over a period of centuries. But now, the building had been restored to all its glory—a great stone and stained-glass edifice.

We were welcomed in the side entrance and showed where to put our luggage while we walked and toured the ageless structure. On one wall was a plaque that listed all the Abbots through the years from 1069 and the Vicars from 1625 to present.

I pointed to the large hanging.

"Look. There, at 1263, is one of your long-ago grandfathers—David Cawood. He was Abbot from 1263 to 1270." Katie and Ashlynn nodded their heads and looked away.

"Can we go over to the gift shop?" Ashlynn asked, clearly not as interested in our ancestry as I was.

Sara looked and took a picture with her phone of the wall hanging. "This is wonderful. Such beauty. And a history of a thousand years," she said.

The stained-glass windows on the east end depicted the family tree of Jesus. Just a straight line like mine of the Cawoods. High in the south end was what is known as the Washington Window. It depicts the Coat of Arms of George Washington's ancestors. It is comprised of two red bands and three red stars. It is very similar to the flag of Washington D. C. It is the same coat of arms that George Washington's family brought to America. The window dates from the 14th century.

Granddaughter Ashlynn rushed up to me. "Bobo," that's what they called me, "they said there was a place over there where a leopard could look in. And I'm scared. I don't want to be close to a leopard."

I looked over to the side of the church. I saw where people could climb up and look through a hole. I took Ashlynn's hand and walked over with her. Then I saw a sign. It was a "Lepers' Hole" or "Squint," as they called it. I climbed up and looked through the hole.

"Ashlynn, it's not about a leopard—a big cat. It's where sick people could look through a hole from the outside to see the service. They had leprosy. They couldn't come in as people were afraid they would catch the disease from them."

"What is leprosy?" she asked.

"A very bad skin disease. Not very much here anymore. But still in India and other countries."

After two hours, coffee and snacks, and a few purchases for the granddaughters at the gift shop, we retrieved our luggage and walked to the Bus station on the street. We were looking for the 42 Bus. It wasn't a long wait. Again, a young man and woman helped us onto the bus with our luggage. We paid our fare and sat down.

Selby looked like a nice town with shops, cafes, and a few manufacturing buildings.

"We need to come back and walk through the town some day while we're here," I told Sara. She nodded her approval.

Along the way, I noticed the houses were near the road and all were brick or stone. I saw none of the vinyl siding that is popular in the States. We passed a cemetery and church. I was amazed at the size of the gravestones.

Then I saw a road sign that said "Cawood" in large block letters. I gently elbowed Sara. "We are about there."

Then we passed a restaurant on our right that had a sign, "Castle Inn."

"We might want to eat there tonight," I said, and Sara nodded

Just one more turn and a half mile later, the bus came to a stop immediately in front of Cawood Castle, or what remained of it, our destination.

We alighted off the bus and took in a view of the Castle Gatehouse. We opened the gate near the road and walked toward the three-story structure. I had a combination to retrieve the key from the lockbox near the door.

The granddaughters looked up at the towering stone structure. "Are we staying here?" Katie asked.

"Yes. You have your own room and own beds," I said, and they nodded their grudging approval.

The rooms were just as they were pictured on Landmark Trust's internet site. Sara and I would be on the second floor in the room that spanned the gatehouse from north to south. Windows were on both sides, with a small kitchen off the back. A bathroom was just five steps down the ancient stone spiral staircase. We had a large four-poster bed. A fireplace faced toward the bed, with two overstuffed chairs facing each other near the fireplace.

"Remind me to buy a bundle of firewood when we go out," I told Sara. "It may get cool in here tonight."

The granddaughters would sleep one floor above us in a similar-sized room with two twin beds. There was another small bathroom off the spiral staircase between our floor and theirs. I thought the girls might not care for walking up the narrow staircase, but they seemed to enjoy the challenge of navigating the steps.

After we got settled and unpacked, I suggested we walk around a bit before dark. We could look out our windows and see a lot of the village, and on the south side was the grassy acreage that was called the Garth.

We began our adventure by turning the corner and walking toward our right. A block down and across the street was a pub named The Ferry Inn. There was a sign advertising games for later in the week. I stepped inside to see what it was like while Sara and the girls waited outside. There were a couple of boards on the wall telling some of the history of Cawood. One detailed "The Great Feast" at the Castle that took place around 1466. It was given by a new Archbishop of York who lived at the castle. He wanted his banquet to be larger than the one given for the new King's coronation.

I read the list of all the items served and the animals and sea creatures that were slaughtered and cooked for the ostentatious occasion. The feast went on for a week. There was no poverty of wine, with over twenty-five hundred gallons being provided. I shook my head. There must have been a lot of drunkenness at this orgy of food and wine.

I walked back out onto the narrow sidewalk and thought we would be lucky to get anything to cook in our small kitchen. It must have been a wonder to behold to have attended that feast nearly six hundred years before.

Cars could barely pass on the street without edging toward the sidewalk. We walked back toward the river bridge. Then we turned around and walked back up the street. A block and a half away, there was another pub named the Jolly Sailor. It was almost adjacent to the castle gatehouse. I wondered if both pubs serving alcohol would eliminate us from taking Ashlynn and Katie in. I would have to ask.

The girls wanted to see the river, so we turned and walked back toward the bridge. When we got there, we could see the River Ouse.

"Can we go swimming or fishing in the river?" Katie asked.

"No," I answered. "The church is just a bit down that way," I said and pointed toward the walkway along the river. "We'll go there sometime this week."

"Another church?" Katie protested.

Walking back up the street to go to the castle, we did stop at what I thought was an odd name for a store--"The Pickled Postie." Turned out it was a combination of a post office, grocery store, and café. There wasn't a huge selection of canned goods and other food items but enough for us to have for sandwiches and snacks. I could also buy a bundle of wood there for our fireplace, which I did.

I looked at the small café seating area. "Do you serve dinner?"

"No, just breakfast, mainly. And you must reserve a place the day before."

I looked at Sara. "Breakfast here in the morning?"

"Yes, that would be nice."

"There'll be four of us," I told the young lady behind the counter.

"Name?" she asked.

"Cawood," I said.

"Oh, I know where we are. I just need your name."

"Cawood is our name. My ancestors are from here. We came over to see what it's like."

"Oh, how wonderful! Where are you staying?"

"The castle gatehouse."

"Oh, that looks spooky. Hope you don't see any ghosts."

I looked at my granddaughters, hoping they didn't hear the word "ghosts."

She wrote our name down for breakfast. We paid for a bag of groceries and a bundle of wood.

Back at the castle, we checked the time and decided to go to the Castle Inn for dinner.

We walked back down Thorpe Lane and turned left onto Wistowgate. It was not far down that street. The sun was still up but hanging low over the western horizon. We didn't have a reservation, but we were seated after a brief fifteen-minute wait.

There was quite a selection on the menu. I had fish and chips. Sara ordered chicken in a basket, and, of course, the granddaughters decided on burgers and fries.

Sara and I shared the Warm Chocolate Brownie for dessert. The girls each got a bowl of ice cream.

"That was delicious," I said when we got back outside.

"Yes," Sara said. "We'll have to come back."

By the time we got back to the castle gate, the sun had gone below the horizon. It was cloudy but not raining. The stone gatehouse stood in a somber, darkening, and austere grey.

The girls stared up at the stark stone building.

"That's creepy looking," Ashlynn said. "Are there any ghosts in there?"

"Not that I know of," I said.

Chapter Two

Servant

With a fire started in the fireplace from the wood I had bought, Sara and I sat down in the two armchairs with our feet up facing the sparkling embers.

"This is the life," I said. "Sitting in a castle with my queen by my side."

"You haven't bought me a crown yet," Sara answered.

Katie and Ashlynn ran down from their room above us. "There's no television and we can barely get anything on our phones or games. What kind of place is this?" Katie asked.

"You'll have to rough it," I answered. "Pretend it's five hundred years ago."

"Ugh!" Katie moaned, and they both turned and ran back up the spiral staircase.

"Get plenty of sleep," I yelled after them. "We're going to York tomorrow. I hear there's a large outlet mall nearby."

With the girls settled in, Sara and I drifted into different realms while sipping cups of tea. I got my notebook and started refreshing my mind on when and how the castle was built and about the people who had lived or visited here. Sara had found some recent magazines left by other guests and was thumbing through them.

From my notes, I saw that at least four kings had visited, beginning with Henry III in 1255; then Edward I in 1299; Edward II in 1314; and King Henry VIII in 1541. He came with Queen Catherine Howard and Thomas Culpepper. There were several Archbishops of York who had lived here. Cardinal Thomas Wolsey had been sent to York and Cawood Castle when King Henry VIII became dissatisfied with him in 1529.

"Oh, I wish these walls could talk," I said to Sara.

"Was this gatehouse always part of the castle?" she asked.

I turned a page in my notes. "No, the castle was built in degrees. First as a manor, then a palace, then transformed into a quadrangular castle. The gatehouse wasn't built until about 1426 by Archbishop John Kemp."

"Then, why is the gatehouse and the adjoining building all that's left?" Sara asked.

"The English Civil War in the 1640s and 1650s," I answered. The Parliamentarians and the Royalists fought with each occupying the castle at different times. After the war, they left the castle to decline—or 'slighted'--as they termed it. A lot of the stone was carried off to build other structures. The Parliamentarians won and they executed King Charles by beheading."

"Wow!" Sara said. "Why couldn't they just have sent him to France or somewhere?"

"Afraid he would return, I guess," I answered.

It had been a long day. The four-poster bed looked inviting. The flames in the fireplace were dying down. It was time to get some rest. Tomorrow would be a busy day too. I walked up the stairs to the granddaughters' room to check on them. Both were snug in their beds and asleep. When I returned, Sara was already in bed. I turned off the lights and joined her.

It seemed like I was asleep immediately. When I next turned over, I grabbed my phone from beside the bed to see what time it was—3 a.m. The fire had dried the air, and I was thirsty. I eased out of bed so as not to awaken Sara and walked softly to the small kitchen adjacent to the bedroom. With just the light sifting through the windows I was able to go to the refrigerator and retrieve a bottled water.

Just as I closed the refrigerator door, I heard what sounded like static from a radio. Was it from Sara's phone or mine? It reminded me of the times in my youth that I would try to tune in a far-away radio station on my transistor radio. I grabbed the door facing with one hand while holding the water bottle in my other.

I looked around the corner to see if I could determine where the raspy sound was coming from. Maybe the dying embers in the fireplace were crackling.

But when I looked toward the fireplace, I was startled by what I saw. In the chair where Sara had sat, there appeared sparkling lines that were emitting light and sound. As I gazed, the strings of light appeared to be what I first thought to be sparklers that we celebrated with on holidays. But they were joined in a strange pattern. They curved and extended to form what looked like the image of a person sitting in the chair. Beginning at the head and extending to feet at the floor, it was fascinating. It wasn't solid—just a lighted outline.

I rubbed my eyes to be sure I was awake. Was this real? It was still there. Now the sparklers had disappeared, and the image appeared translucent. I could see through it. The hand moved and then a foot tapped the floor. It was a man. He was wearing clothes that would have been worn by men hundreds of years ago.

He glanced my way and motioned for me to sit in the other chair. I couldn't speak, but I followed his directions. I was startled, but somehow, I wasn't afraid.

When I sat down and turned toward him, I could see he was smiling. I thought to myself, "Who are you?"

Without me actually mouthing the question, he looked at me and I heard his answer.

"I am Servant."

Again, I thought to myself, "How did he know what I was thinking?"

"We communicate by mental telepathy," I heard his words.

I remained silent, but thought, "Mental telepathy? How does that work? Are you a ghost?"

"We prefer 'spirit' to 'ghost.' I have no physical presence that you can touch. But I can hear what you're thinking. And my thinking the answer will be like sounds in your brain."

I was beginning to get the gist of this way of communicating. I thought, "Can my wife hear or see you?"

"No, just you and me unless I decide that someone else can be in my presence."

"Why are you called 'Servant'?" I asked in my thoughts.

"Let me tell you my story," I heard his words. "I was a servant here at the castle for seventy years. My physical body lived here from 1453 until my death at age ninety in 1543. I outlived most of my contemporaries. It was unusual for someone to live to ninety at that time. My Spirit still remains in this area most of the time.

"The Great Spirit allows me to travel about as I wish, but I like it here. I became a servant at the age of twelve when they needed so many workers for The Great Feast."

I put my hand to my mouth. I was afraid to say anything or even think anything since he could read my mind. But finally, I decided to think a question. "Can you tell me about The Great Feast?"

"Yes, I can. But it would be better if I invited Archbishop George Neville to tell you about it."

"You can bring him here?" I thought.

"The Great Spirit sent him to London, but I believe I can get him to come here tomorrow. His being sent to London is part of the full story. But I'll tell you about what I remember of The Great Feast of 1465."

"By the way, Servant," I thought, "why did you come to see me?"

Did I detect a smile on his shadowy face?

"I saw you at the Ferry Inn looking at the board about The Great Feast, and I knew you were staying here. So, I thought I would come and visit. It is rare that I make my presence known."

"You stay at the castle all of the time?"

"Oh, no. I go to All Saints' Church, the Ferry Inn, the Jolly Sailor, the Castle Inn, and other places around here. I visit York and Selby. Just about any place I want to go."

"But nobody sees you?"

"Just occasionally.

"Now back to what I know about The Great Feast. You see, I was twelve years old. George Neville was from a very rich and prominent family. They were well connected with royalty. He wanted a feast celebrating his ascension to Archbishop of York to be grander than the king's coronation party.

"And it was. Practically every able-bodied man, woman, and child were conscripted to work preparing for the feast. There were cattle, pigs, ducks, geese, swans, pheasants, deer, does, bucks, pigeons, peacocks—even porpoises and seals. What you see out there as the Garth was where we held most of those animals waiting to be slaughtered.

"We had numerous butchers and cooks. The waste was hauled off to the river. I just did whatever I was told. There were thousands of gallons of wine. A lot of men got drunk—and women. Even I, a twelve-year-old, had my first taste of wine."

"How many people were there?" I thought.

"There were over six hundred invited guests. But I would say it was more like six thousand who came. Everybody in the village. Most were working like I was, but others came for the food. Neville didn't care. 'The more the merrier' would have been his response."

"How long did it go on?"

"A week or more. There was a lot of drunkenness. I know of two men who died."

"What happened to them?"

"Too much wine and food, I guess. It sounds funny now, but we loaded them up into the wagon we used to haul off the waste and took their bodies down to All Saints Church and laid them in the graveyard."

"Did you bury them?"

"We didn't. I guess somebody did."

I looked over toward the window where the garth lay outside. "So, you dumped the guts and waste from the butchered animals into the Ouse?"

"Yes. All the dogs from the village would follow the wagons waiting for scraps to fall off. Some of the dogs would jump onto the wagons. They rolled around among the guts and excrement. Smelly lot of dogs. That's where the term, 'Smells like a dog off a gut wagon' comes from.

"I would go upstream and wash off in the river because I was starting to smell like some of those dogs."

"Oh, my," I thought. "And you can get George Neville's ghost here tomorrow?"

"Spirit of George Neville."

"Okay. What about the others? Like the kings who visited? Thomas Wolsey? The other archbishops?"

"Yes. All of them—probably one at a time. And with the Great Spirit's permission."

"Do I need to do anything?"

"Start another fire for when I come back tomorrow with George."

I nodded my head. When I looked back, he was gone. I put both hands on my head. Had this been a dream? I looked at my phone. It was 4 a.m. I had been up for an hour.

I went to the bed and eased in, not wanting to wake Sara. But she awoke anyway.

"Where've you been?" she asked.

"Just had to go get a drink," I said. I didn't believe she or the girls were ready for ghost stories. I would determine if it was real the next night.

Chapter Three

George Neville

Four hours of fitful sleep from 4 a.m. to 8 a.m. didn't seem sufficient. But because I talked with a ghost—or spirit—as Servant preferred to be called, sound sleep hadn't come easily. The wood in the fireplace was just ashes now.

We were scheduled for breakfast at the Pickled Postie. I rousted Katie and Ashlynn awake with promises of what they wanted for their meal.

The short walk from the castle to the Pickled Postie in the crisp May morning air was refreshing. But my mind kept returning to my conversation—as it was—with Servant in the wee hours of the morning. Was he really going to bring the ghost—spirit—of George Neville back to the castle in the early hours of morning? If he did, what would I do, ask, or think?

We were seated in the back of the café area. I wanted bacon and scrambled eggs. Did they have that in England? The girls ordered hot cakes or the English equivalent. Sara took a muffin and coffee. They did have coffee or tea. I took coffee also.

There was a constant ebb and flow of locals coming to do business at the post office or to buy some necessities. A few came toward the back to the other two tables to eat breakfast. When they saw us, they usually nodded or tipped their hats. "A friendly lot," I thought. "They're probably wondering who these strangers are."

I knew I needed another bundle of firewood for tonight, but I decided to wait and buy it when we returned from York.

We walked the short distance to where the 42 Bus had its stop in front of the castle and waited. The bus was practically full when it stopped for us. But the obliging passengers made room for us. We all found seats but not together. The bus turned and crossed the bridge over the River Ouse and into the countryside.

It was a beautiful area—low lying farmland with horses grazing. We passed two girls riding their horses on the side of the road. Ashlynn pointed to them. "Can I ride a horse today?"

"Probably not today, but maybe later in the week."

The bus passed the Grey Horse at Kelfield, Village Hall, and the small town of Fulford on our way to York. The stop at the Outlet Mall saw most of the passengers get off for a day of shopping. I pointed toward the mall. "You girls can go shopping there tomorrow."

We rode on to the Picadilly stop in downtown York. We had already purchased tickets for the double-decker sight-seeing tour bus in York. We would take a lap around York and decide what to see. I looked at my phone at the time. It had only been a forty-minute ride with all the stops to go from Cawood Castle to downtown York.

On the drive around York on the second floor of the tour bus, we all saw things we wanted to come back to. There was a commentary we listened to which described some of the history of York and the works we were seeing. At one point we passed through the stone city wall. The passage looked almost the same as the Cawood Castle Gatehouse. The speaker said we could walk along the city wall all around most of the town. The trek would take about two hours. We got off the bus near a big hill that supported a rounded former castle.

The girls pointed to Clifford's Tower. "Can we go up there?" Katie asked.

I stared at the fifty-five steps up to the main area. "Why don't you and Ashlynn walk up while your Nana and I wait down here on a park bench. Then we'll walk over to the York Castle Museum which is just across the yard."

They agreed and took off up the steps running after I gave them the entry fare. Sara and I sat on the bench and enjoyed the mid-morning sunshine. I looked at a brochure I had which listed some of the attractions in York.

I was especially interested in visiting York Minster which was the home church of the Archbishop of York. I was wondering why the archbishops during the 1400s and 1500s chose to live at Cawood Castle rather than somewhere nearer the York Minster. It was about ten miles from York to Cawood Castle. Riding a horse or horse-pulled coach could be a half-day's trip. Maybe they wanted to get away from all the religious trappings and have a more relaxing time at the castle.

I looked on my phone to research while we sat on the bench. I found that the present-day Archbishops lived at Bishopthorpe Palace which had been purchased by Archbishop Walter de Gray in 1226. It was added to as a Manor House and became a palace later. It was just south of York. I thought of history and the Viking invasions. Then there were different revolts. Perhaps the archbishops felt safer at Cawood Castle rather than facing the prospects of war in York. That could be a question I could pose to George Neville if he showed up at the Gatehouse with Servant in the dark morning hours.

When the girls came down from Clifford's Tower, we walked toward the York Castle Museum.

"That Clifford's Tower was neat," Katie said. "I'm beginning to like history I'll have plenty of info to write papers with for school in the fall."

"That's great," I said, "since we had to agree this was an informational and cultural trip to take you out of school in May—a month before school ended."

The museum housed exhibits that were almost like what life was like in the centuries before. We walked through and around horse and carriage figures. Furniture from the different eras was on display. On the far side of the museum, we walked through what had been a "debtors" prison.

"They put people in jail for not paying what they owed?" Ashlyn asked.

"I'm afraid so," I said.

"That was mean," she answered.

From the museum, we walked up and around to the Yorkshire Museum. I knew from my research that a Viking sword was on display there. It was called the Cawood Sword because it had been found in the River Ouse near Cawood in the 1800s and probably dates from the 1200s. It had been held at the Tower of London for a long period until 1950 when it was sold to a private collector. Finally, it came into possession of the Yorkshire Museum. It was noted as probably the finest Viking sword ever found.

When we looked at it through the glass enclosure, we were not disappointed.

"If it's the Cawood Sword, why can't you take it home with you? You're a Cawood," Ashlynn asked.

"Well, it doesn't belong to our family. It's called the Cawood Sword because it was found in the river near the Cawood Castle," I answered.

"You should claim it. File a lawsuit or something," Katie said. "You're a lawyer."

I shook my head. Katie was on track to be a litigator.

A visit to the York Minster would have to await until a later day. The girls wanted to see the National Railway Museum. We got back on the tour bus and rode toward the railway museum. It was just a short walk from the bus stop. And best of all, the museum was free. But I did make a donation.

The granddaughters enjoyed the railway museum more than I thought they would. While I enjoyed seeing the old passenger cars, dining cars, and engines, I wondered whether they would be bored. But they walked briskly from one exhibit to another.

"That was great," Ashlynn said when we left. "But you know what I want to see next?"

"No. What?"

"The Viking Museum."

I looked at my phone. It was too late to go today. "Not today, Ashlynn. Some day later this week. It's time to eat and get back to the castle before we miss the last bus."

"There's a McDonald's," Katie said when we got back to downtown York.

"No," I said. "We didn't come all the way to England to eat at a McDonald's."

After we ate at a local restaurant, we caught the 42 bus to go back to the Gatehouse. We walked from the stop in front of the castle back to the Pickled Postie, where I bought another bundle of wood for the fireplace. We also bought some pancake mix, butter, bacon, and milk to cook our own breakfast the next morning.

After I got the wood in the fireplace lit, I pulled two more chairs up to face the fire.

"What are you doing?" Sara asked.

"I thought the girls might want to sit for a while," I said, while in the back of my mind I knew I was preparing another chair for George Neville's appearance. Maybe he would bring someone with him to occupy the other chair.

After an hour of sitting in front of the fire, the girls ran up to their room. I looked at my phone before going to bed and set a vibrating alarm for fifteen minutes before Servant was to arrive with Neville.

I was vibrated awake as scheduled with the phone by my ear. I slipped out of bed and went to the kitchen for a bottle of water. I looked around the corner toward the chairs and fireplace, but Servant wasn't there. I tiptoed to the third chair and sat. I poked the embers to get the fire up for a bit.

When I looked at the chair where Servant had sat previously, he appeared in a sparkling radiance. I began to think my mental telepathy questions.

"How are you?"

"Pretty good for a six-hundred-years-old spirit."

"Will George Neville be joining us?'

"In a bit. He's on his way from London."

"Well, may I ask you some questions about my ancestors who lived during your physical lifetime?"

"Yes. I knew three of your 'grandfathers' during that time. They were not very original with their name selection. All three were named John. The first John was thirty when we had The Great Feast. He came to it. His son, John, was born ten years after the feast. And the third John wasn't born until I was in my sixties."

"Did they all visit the castle?"

"Yes, but they mainly lived down the road at Keesbury. It was their home—their manor."

"Were they good people?"

"Yes. Extraordinary. Their ancestors had been keepers of the King's forests for several hundred years. That's why their Coat of Arms has three harts' heads on the shield. They made sure that the royalty could come here as a hunting headquarters. The ordinary people couldn't hunt the deer—just the hares."

"Anything special about them?"

"Oh, yes. The grandson, John, was brilliant. He studied with the priests. He was able to read Latin and Greek. He had learned about those new-fangled devices called printing presses. The year before I died that young John Cawood took off for London where they had printing presses. I understand he did quite well there and became the printer for Queen Mary and Queen Elizabeth."

"Yes," I thought. "He is buried beneath St. Paul's Cathedral in London."

"There's another Cawood buried under All Saints' Church here in Cawood. I can go with you tomorrow to visit his spirit. He hangs around the church most of the time."

"Yes. I would like to do that. Anybody else interesting buried at the Church?"

"Yes. One Archbishop is buried there. He was born here at Cawood about twenty-five years after I died. George Montaigne is his name. Everybody called him 'Big Mountain'. Unfortunately, he died just four months after being installed as Archbishop. He served from July 1628 until his death in October 1628."

"You know a lot of archbishops?"

"Ha, ha. I've had a lot of time to know them or learn about them."

Just then a floating sparkling apparition appeared above the chair beside Servant and settled into it.

"Welcome, George," I heard Servant say. "It's about time you got here."

"It was a little trip from London, and I had to get permission from the Great Spirit. Is this who you were telling me about?" he said and pointed a sparkling finger at me.

"Yes," I heard Servant respond. "This is Mr. Chris Cawood. He is a descendant of the Cawoods from here in the village. He's just learning how to communicate with us through mental telepathy."

Then I heard in my mind the voice of George Neville again. "Good to meet you. Some of your ancestors came to that little party I put on. They were good people. What would you like to ask me or talk about?"

"About the Feast, or 'little party' as you called it. And why are you in London and not here?"

I could see the outline of Neville's hands slapping his knees.

"London! That's what I'd like to know. It was all about the party. The Great Spirit sent me to London. I have been consigned to the kitchen of what was an insane asylum since I died in 1476. The Great Spirit said I had to do penance for my 'ostentatious' feast. That's what He called it--'ostentatious'."

"Well, it was rather elaborate."

"Ha, ha, larger and better than the king's coronation. I had more notables here than he had. If I remember correctly, there were fifty-nine knights, ten abbots, seven bishops, numerous lawyers, clergy, esquires and ladies. I put many people to work—cooks, butchers, horsemen, hunters, boatmen. Servant here worked for me at the feast. He was but a young lad.

"I fed over six thousand. That's what I told the Great Spirit. I said, 'I fed six thousand while your Son only fed five thousand.'"

"What did the Great Spirit say to that?" I asked.

"He said my purpose and intent were not righteous. Can you believe that? Saying an archbishop's purpose and intent were not 'righteous'?"

"What about the amount of wine and ale? My research says three hundred tuns of ale and two hundred fifty tuns of wine. If a tun was 252 gallons, that meant there were seventy-five thousand six hundred gallons of ale and sixty-three thousand gallons of wine."

"Well, we had some left over for me and the regular staff. And my guests and all the people from the village had a good time. No one complained."

"And the food—2000 chickens, 104 peacocks, 1200 quail, 400 swans, 113 oxen, six wild bulls, 12 porpoises and seals, 1000 sheep, 304 calves, 2000 pigs, 4000 mallards and teals, 200 pheasants, 500 stags, bucks, and roes, 4000 cold and 1500 hot venison pies, 4000 dishes of jelly, 4000 baked tarts, 2000 hot custards, bread, cakes and other delicacies. I could see how someone could call that 'ostentatious'," I said.

"Everybody to their own opinion, I guess."

I looked at some notes I was holding. "You were also Chancellor of England until the king got angry with you."

"Yes. He took away the great seal and demoted me. Put me in prison. You just didn't know which side to be on back then—who was going to win. Edward IV and Henry VI. I tried to be on the winning side, but it wasn't to be. The War of the Roses was going on. They put me in prison in the Tower and then in France. France wasn't bad, but every day at the Tower I looked out the window to see if they were getting the chopping block ready for me."

"You had a very notable career. It's good to live in interesting times," I said. "How did you get to be archbishop of York?"

"Our family was highly connected. My brother was known as 'The King Maker'. I had to have the blessings of the Pope and King to be appointed. Archbishop was second in importance to the king. That was my view. Archbishop of Canterbury and Archbishop of York.

"It was a very lucrative position. I can say it now. I sold a lot of bishop and abbot positions. A lot of money. I was wealthy to start with. I became very wealthy."

"Why did you choose to live here at Cawood Castle rather than in York?"

"This was much nicer. They had that Bishopthorpe Palace. But it wasn't as much of a palace as a manor. Practically all the Archbishops of York lived here. When I was here, there was a banqueting hall, at least two other dining rooms, a library, and much more than there was at York.

"Besides, at York, I had to wade through all the beggars, lame people, and even those with leprosy who waited outside the Minster for money or some healing miracle. Cawood Castle was the place to be. There was also civil strife going on around York from time to time. Here I had castle walls and the gatehouse for protection. From the 1300s, most of the archbishops lived here."

"And several died here," I heard Servant say.

I looked at my notes again. "You died when you were about forty-three. Why so young?"

"I don't know. Either someone poisoned me or a heart attack, as you modern people call it. I'm sure it wasn't from overeating and drinking at the feast. Ha, ha."

Servant sat there silently. He then turned toward me. "I believe we better let the archbishop get back to London."

"Thank you for coming," I said. He vanished up toward the ceiling.

"A great partier," Servant said. "Shall we meet at All Saints' Church this afternoon around 3 p.m. to see your ancestor, John, and maybe go to the Selby Abbey to see your ancestor, David?"

"I think I can arrange to be there," I said. When I looked up, Servant was gone.

Chapter Four

All Saints Church and Selby Abbey

We slept in a bit later that morning. I decided I would have to tell my wife about my visits with ghosts—or spirits. But how would I do that without her thinking me crazy? At least she might send me to what had been the insane asylum where George Neville was doing his penance. I certainly couldn't mention it to my granddaughters. They would be scared to death.

I got up and looked out the window toward the Garth. There were no sheep today. I started the coffee in the kitchen and made my way up the stairs to the girls' room.

"Breakfast downstairs in a half hour," I said as I walked by the entrance to their room and up the stairway toward the roof. There were a couple of folding chairs near the door leading out. I might use them later if Servant, and I got together on the roof instead of in front of the fireplace.

It was still cool with a bit of wind when I walked out. I stepped over to the Garth side of the top of the gatehouse. Looking down and into the distance, I could imagine what it must have been like in the 1400s and 1500s when mounted horsemen and carriages brought notables to the castle.

I remembered reading that when Cardinal Wolsey was arrested and taken away on his own mule, thousands gathered in the Garth to wish him goodbye. A lot of the King's men and a lot of the King's horses couldn't put Cardinal Wolsey back together again when he died at Leicester on his way to London to be imprisoned in the Tower and probably to lose his head.

Then it struck me. I must ask Servant to bring Wolsey back to the castle for a meeting. Servant was certainly living up to his name or title. He was always helpful in bringing the spirits back for a meeting. Today it was to be two of my ancestors. David Cawood, who had been Abbot of Selby in 1263, was the grandfather of John, who lived from 1322 to 1390 and was buried beneath the floor of All Saints Church here in the Village of Cawood.

"I liked having breakfast at that pickle place yesterday," Ashlynn said when I got back to the kitchen.

"The Pickled Postie," I said. "But this will be nice to cook our own breakfast. We'll eat here and plan our day around the table."

"When can we go shopping at that mall?" Katie asked.

I looked across the table at Sara. "That would be a good thing for you girls to do today. A day off from visiting churches and historical stuff. You can catch the 42 bus and get off at the mall."

"But I still want to see the Viking Museum," Ashlynn said.

"Yes, we can do that later in the week," I said.

"What are you going to do?" Sara asked me.

"I'll probably walk around the village, review my genealogy notes some more, and may ride the 42 up to Selby to see if I can find out any more about my ancestor who was an Abbot at the Abbey. Maybe they have some preserved papers of his."

"From 1200? I doubt it," Sara said.

So that was the plan. The girls would be off shopping. I told them to be back before dark, and we could eat dinner at the Castle Inn.

I would wander around and be sure to be at All Saints Church to meet Servant at 3 p.m. If he turned up with my ancestor John, I could be certain that my visits were not nighttime dreams. We were going to meet in broad daylight. And if Servant showed up, I would have to find a way to tell Sara about my experiences. I had kept it from her long enough.

They checked the schedule for the 42 Bus and walked to the stop just outside the gatehouse at 10 a.m. I stood with them until the bus came and they got on, happy to go shopping.

I turned and walked back toward the gatehouse. But this time I went to my left and around what was called the banqueting hall toward the grassy Garth. Through a small gate and to the right stood a sign describing the Garth and the footpaths that led through it. There were two ponds supposedly used in past centuries to keep fish to be cooked at the castle. A quarry pit, garden area, and orchard were depicted on the sign.

The path led me across the Bishopdyke and onto Sherburn Street. Turning right, I walked past houses and then onto where the Jolly Sailor Pub was located. It was too early for it to be opened, but I looked through the window anyway. I wondered whether Servant was watching me. No, I hoped he was getting ready for our visit to the church at 3 p.m.

On down the street at the corner, I was back to the Pickled Postie. Although I needed nothing, I stepped in and went to the Post counter.

"Could I buy an envelope with you stamping the name of the Post Office on it?" I asked. "I want a souvenir with the Cawood stamp on it." She obliged, and I now had an envelope with Cawood on it as the location of its being posted. The tables were vacant, so I sat and had a cup of coffee.

A gentleman came up to me, smiled, and said, "I hear you're a Cawood and staying at the gatehouse. I'm John Cattanach. I live just across from the gatehouse. I'm a Councillor for Cawood and Wistow, or at least I am until they change everything."

I reached out my hand. "Good to meet you, John. What a lovely village. My wife and granddaughters are on their way to the Outlet Mall near York to shop. I'm just walking around a bit."

"Well, if you need anything while you're here, just look me up. The people here at the Postie can ring me up. How far have you traced your ancestors back here?"

"Twenty-two generations to the 1200s."

"That's mighty great. I'll let you get on with it. May see you around some more." And with that, he turned and walked out the door. People here are so friendly and nice to a stranger from America, I thought.

When I finished my coffee, I resumed my stroll around town. I turned right out the door and walked toward the bridge and river. Across the street, I could see a building with a sign that said The Ferry Inn. I looked both ways and stepped across the street. Again, when I arrived at the door to The Ferry Inn, it was closed. Too early for a pub, I thought.

Turning back toward the bridge, I could see the River Ouse. I remembered from my research that the Cawood Sword of Viking origin was found near here. At one time, over sixty Viking long boats docked along the river on their way to York. That would have been a sight to behold—if they didn't rob and kill you.

I found a bench and sat down. It was still too early to meet Servant at All Saints' Church. What would I ask John Cawood, who died in 1390? I didn't have a piece of paper on which to write any questions. I had folded the postal envelope and put it in my back pocket. Every few minutes, I looked at my phone to see what time it was. I was eager for a daytime meeting with Servant.

Getting up from the bench, I walked down the sidewalk that paralleled the river. It was about a half mile to the church. When I arrived. I was still an hour early. I walked around the surrounding cemetery and viewed every headstone. Some were very old. "Ann Kingston," said one. "Wife of David Kingston, departed this life on 26th day of October, 1854, Aged 71 years."

When I came to the right back wall of the church, I saw the engraving in the stone of the Cawood Coat of Arms and the Acclom Coat of Arms, which proclaimed the marriage of Margaret Cawood and Robert Acclom in the 1400s. Both families must have been prominent to have their coats of arms chiseled into the church's wall. I knew part of the building dated from the late 1100s.

Although early, I stepped to the door to see if I could enter. Maybe Servant was there early too. No, it was locked. I knocked lightly and stepped back. In a moment, I heard the door lock turn from the inside. "Good," I thought, "Servant is here."

When the door opened, an older lady peered through the opening. "Yes," she said. "May I help you?"

"Oh," I said. "I was wondering if I could come in and see the inside."

She smiled. "Certainly. All Saints is always open for the interested and worshipful." She then opened the door wider to allow my entrance.

I explained to her about my Cawood heritage and that I had an ancestor buried under the floor.

"We have Archbishop George Montaigne buried inside, and a few others. But I don't know exactly where, since the floor has coverings over most of it," she said.

"He died in 1390," I said.

"That was before my time," she said and laughed.

I looked around at the interior. "This is a lovely place," I said. "May I sit for a while and meditate and pray?" I asked.

"Of course. Make yourself at home. I'm going to be in the rear arranging some crafts for a fair we're having later in the month."

I chose a pew in the front and sat down midway across, leaving room for Servant on one side and John Cawood on the other.

It was only a few minutes before I looked to my right. There was Servant in all his sparkly splendor. "Remember, communicate by telepathy," he thought, and I heard. "Don't speak using your physical voice."

I nodded, and then I thought, "I believed you opened the door for me until I saw that lady."

"No. We spirits cannot and do nothing physical. We are only spiritual beings. Nothing physical in presence or in doing anything. You could put your hand right through me. What you see is just an apparition. There are thousands of spirits around here. If we did physical things, it would be utter chaos."

"So, you are not angels."

"No. They are a whole different breed. They existed with the Great Spirit before we were ever born physically or became spirits."

Just then, I looked to my left. There was another spirit. He was not as golden and sparkly as Servant. His appearance was more like steel or aluminum wire wrapped around a statue.

"Chris, meet your ancestor, John," I heard Servant say. "John, this is your Cawood descendant, Chris."

The figure appeared to bow slightly. "Glad to meet another Cawood. You're from America? We didn't even know where that was when I lived here."

"You lived from1322 until 1390, is that correct?" I asked.

"If you say so. We didn't have many calendars back then."

"Why the church burial?" I asked.

"The Cawood family were great benefactors to the church. We even had our own chapel room over there where the coat of arms is engraved on what is now the outside wall, but at one time was part of the inside chapel wall."

"Quite a history," I thought and looked over at Servant, who was motionless. "Why were you buried here inside the church instead of in the cemetery outside?" I asked through my thoughts.

"Ha, ha. My wife's decision. She said I should go to church more. So, she had me buried under the floor. I'm now here for every service."

"We're going to Selby later to visit your grandfather, David," I said.

"Yes. He died before I was born. I've only met him in spirit. A great man. Was Abbot of Selby Abbey."

"And your grandson, John, had a daughter who was married here," I said.

"Yes. I died physically before that grandson was born. But I came to his daughter's wedding here at the church—in spirit."

"Do you stay around the church most of the time?"

"Most of the time. But I go to other places. I used to go to the castle when I was physically alive. I went to the feast in spirit when your buddy, Servant, helped out with Neville's big party. I go to Selby and York occasionally. This is a nice, quiet place where I like to stay."

"Anybody else buried here that I would know?"

"Yes. George Montaigne was buried about two hundred thirty years after me. I call him 'Big Mountain.' An interesting and humble guy. He was born here in Cawood. Got to be Archbishop of York. But he died after about four months. He's the only archbishop buried here, although quite a few died at the castle. Most wanted to be buried at the York Minster."

"Is he here today?"

"No. He went up to York to visit at the Minster."

I looked at my phone for the time. "Well, I'd better catch the 42 and go up to Selby to see your grandfather," I said and looked to Servant, who nodded his approval.

I heard John say, "Goodbye. And say 'Hello' to my grandfather for me." When I looked back to my left, he was gone.

"I'll walk up and catch the 42 bus," I told Servant. I stood and told the lady in the back that I was leaving. I thanked her for her courtesy.

"I'll go with you," I heard Servant say. His golden image traveled along with me as I walked out.

"I'm going to ride the bus," I told Servant through my thoughts.

"I'll ride with you," he said. "I don't have to pay a fare."

"Because you're so old?"

"No. Because nobody can see me—except you."

I nodded and looked down at Servant. His toes barely touched the sidewalk. He just floated along. He was barely five feet tall, in my estimation.

We didn't have to wait long at the bus stop near the gatehouse. I got on and paid my fare. Servant followed. I found two seats together. Servant sat next to the window with me by the aisle.

"You ride the bus very often?" I thought.

"No. Just occasionally," I heard Servant answer.

We both got off at Number 4 station in Selby, which was close to the Abbey.

"Have you made arrangements with David to meet us?" I queried.

"Yes. He said to go in and have a seat on a pew near the front and he would join us. He's here most of the time."

The Abbey did not have many visitors at this time of day. All who were there kept a reverential quiet tone in their voices. We took seats in a pew near the front from which I could see the Washington Window. Servant sat on my right side again. Shortly, Servant looked at me and pointed to my left. I looked. There was who I thought must be the spirit of David Cawood. His appearance was more like that of Servant—a gold-looking mesh that flowed around the appearance of a human body.

"Hello, I'm David Cawood. Glad you could visit. I saw you a few days ago when you came through with your family."

"My wife and grandchildren," I answered in my head.

"Yes. One of your granddaughters was afraid there was a leopard looking in. Very funny."

"I remember that."

"Now tell me, how many generations are you removed from me?"

"Twenty-one, if I'm counting correctly."

"So, the Cawood family still exists and in America."

"Yes. Almost in every state. And in South Africa, New Zealand, Australia, Canada, and other places. We have been very prolific."

"Ha, ha. I'm glad that abbots didn't have to take that vow of celibacy like some priests or monks did. Of course, some priests didn't take it too seriously. There was an abbot or two and a few monks or priests who got into trouble. They were accused of not taking care of business here at the abbey—being lazy and inefficient. And they were accused of being involved with what were called 'loose women' of the town. More than one time it happened."

"Oh, a little hanky-panky going on. That's an American phrase," I said.

"Where did you live when you were abbot here—1263 to 1270—isn't that right?"

"Yes, I was just twenty-three when I became abbot. There was that problem with the one before me. So, he was removed and I was installed. He later came back into good graces and became abbot again. I lived here and in a nice manor just up the street. But it has fallen into disrepair now.

"When I left from being abbot, I moved back to our family manor at Keesbury. I had to petition the king to get some of our land back. We—the Cawood family—at one time owned at least a third of the Village of Cawood. We had rights to the fishing in the River Ouse and were keepers of the King's forests."

"Did you ever stay at the Cawood Castle?" I asked.

"Yes. At one time, we occupied the castle. Of course, it wasn't always a castle. It went from a nice manor to a palace and could be called a castle when it was enclosed and gated."

"Did you ever see any prominent people there?"

"Oh, yes. Three kings in succession—Henry III, when I was fifteen years old. Then his son—Edward I. He stayed there about six years on and off while he was fighting the Scots from 1299. He's the one I petitioned to get some of our land back. He obliged—but not in full. Then his son—Edward the II visited with his wife the year before I died. You know, the kings thought of this area as their hunting grounds and the castle as their hunting lodge."

"Very interesting," I thought.

"You ought to get your friend, Servant, to round up the spirits of those three kings and bring them to the castle to talk with."

I looked over at Servant and asked in my mind, "Can you do that?"

Servant hesitated for a moment and then said, "Give me a day or two."

"What were your duties as abbot?" I asked.

"I handled relations with church officials. I saw that the abbey was run properly. I also interacted with the civil officials. Today, you would call me the CEO of the abbey."

David and I chatted for another half hour until I saw they were beginning to close the doors.

"Thanks for visiting with me," I told David. "We had better get out of here before they lock us in."

"They can't lock me in," Servant said.

When we were back on the street on our way to the bus stop, I turned to Servant. "Can you get those three kings to the castle?"

"Give me another day. No meeting this next early morning. But we'll try for the next morning. I know a couple of them still roam up in Scotland. It will take me a bit."

"And how about meeting on the roof of the gatehouse? More room for five of us."

"That would be good. With the stars shining above at 3 a.m."

"Servant, I have been researching all those who lived, visited, or died at the castle. I would like to see them all. Not all at one time. But one or two at a time."

"Who are you speaking of?" Servant asked.

I rubbed my head. I didn't have my paper list with me.

"Cardinal Wolsey, Archbishop John Kemp, Catherine Howard, Thomas Culpeper, all the archbishops who lived and died at the castle, and, of course, King Henry VIII," I said.

"Quite a list and quite a task," Servant said. "Wolsey is in Leicester, about ninety miles away, and Kemp was buried in Canterbury. Catherine Howard and Thomas Culpeper were executed in London. The archbishops were buried at York Minster except for 'Big Mountain', who lies beneath All Saints Church in Cawood.

"Ha, ha, King Henry VIII. He'll be a tough nut to crack. He stays mainly at Hampton Court. He's very arrogant. Thinks he still rules England.

"I'll do my best. But let's start with Henry III, Edward I, and Edward II."

"Ok. Do your best. See you soon on the roof of the gatehouse."

Chapter Five

The Three Kings

"I have been seeing ghosts," I told my wife the next morning. We were sitting at the table in our room in the gatehouse of Cawood Castle, having a second cup of coffee after breakfast. The granddaughters had gone down to walk in the Garth. We were planning another trip to York. Ashlynn wanted to see the Viking Museum, and I wanted to visit York Minster.

Sara smiled and set down her cup of coffee. "You've been having bad dreams?"

"No. I have seen and talked with ghosts of people who stayed here at the castle. They prefer to be called 'spirits,' but they're like ghosts to me."

Sara put her hands together on the table. Her smile changed to an inquisitive look. "Are you joking with me?"

"I know it sounds strange. But for two nights—really early morning—I sat right there and talked with two people who died hundreds of years ago. Then, yesterday I went to All Saints Church and visited with my ancestor who is buried there. Then I took the bus to Selby and sat with David Cawood, who was abbot there in 1263."

"You sat right there by the fireplace and talked to ghosts? At what time?"

"About 3 a.m."

"And you talking didn't wake me where I was sleeping just behind those chairs?"

"That's another thing. They don't talk with voices as you and I do."

"How do they talk, then?" she asked.

"Mental telepathy. What they think—I hear. What I think—they hear."

Sara looked over at the chairs in front of the fireplace. "Is that why you put extra chairs there? So, you could talk to your ghosts? Did they sit down or stand up?"

"Well, one night there were three of us."

"I did wake up one time and saw you sitting there in front of the fireplace. You were moving your hands a little. But I thought you were just warming them in front of the fire. I didn't hear anything, and I certainly didn't see any ghosts."

"No. You couldn't hear them. And you couldn't see them. Only I could see and hear them. It was the same way at the church and at Selby Abbey. They appeared and talked with me but nobody else could see or hear them. Servant even rode the bus with me, and nobody could see him."

"'Servant'! Who is this 'Servant'?"

"Servant is the spirit who first visited me. He worked here at the castle in the 1400s and early 1500s. He lived to be ninety. He is the one who arranged the other visits."

Sara shook her head. "I know a couple of good psychiatrists back in Tennessee. I think you might need to see one when we get back. Are you having any other signs of something happening with your brain?"

"No. I'm fine. I'm kind of excited about seeing these ghosts. Servant is going to bring three kings to the top of the gatehouse tomorrow morning around 3 a.m."

"I think I've heard that song, 'We three kings of Orient are . . . .' Are those the ones he's bringing?"

"No, that's just a Christmas song about the three wise men. He's bringing King Henry III, King Edward I, and King Edward II."

"I would think King Henry VIII would be more interesting. Maybe with a few of his six wives. Of course, a couple of them would have to come with their heads cut off," Sara said.

"That's for a later date. Servant said King Henry VIII likes to stay around Hampton Court and is uppity, aloof, and arrogant. He will be a difficult one to get here."

"Why would they come back here?"

"They all visited or lived here at one time or the other."

"King Henry VIII visited here?"

"Yes, with his Queen Catherine Howard and Thomas Culpeper."

Sara remembered some of the English history. "That didn't turn out well for Catherine or Thomas, did it?"

"I'd say that while Henry was out hunting deer in the forest, Catherine and Thomas were here whispering dear nothings in each other's ears."

Sara stood and walked to the far window to see if she could see the granddaughters. Then she turned back to me. "Don't you think it would be dangerous to go up on the roof of the gatehouse tonight? What if one of these kingly ghosts pushed you off?"

"That can't happen. They can do nothing of a physical nature. They're just spirits. And they are friendly. You remember when we were young there were cartoons about 'Casper, the friendly ghost'?"

"Yes, I remember Casper. It was fiction. Just like these ghosts in your head are fiction. Something is getting into your brain."

"Don't worry. I'll be safe. I'll tell you when I go up and when I come down."

"Don't mention it to Ashlynn or Katie. It would scare them to death to think you are meeting ghosts one level above their room. They'd probably think you're crazy too and ask me to hospitalize you."

We heard the downstairs door open and the girls running up the stairs.

"That Garth is a neat place," Ashlynn said. "There were some funny-looking birds, ducks, and I saw the sheep."

"When are we going back to York?" Katie asked.

I looked at my phone for the time. "The bus should be here in half an hour. Get ready." I glanced at Sara. I didn't think I had convinced her about the ghosts of Cawood Castle.

The 42 Bus was on time, and we got on immediately in front of the fence near the road. We were fortunate that it hadn't rained during our time at Cawood and on our visits to Selby and York. The rural farmland was a lush green. The village sidewalks on the route to York were busy with people walking to stores. The girls wanted to get off again at the outlet mall when the bus stopped and emptied half its passengers.

"No. Not today. You can come back later this week with your grandmother. Today we're going to the. . ." I looked at my notes. "The JORVIK Viking Centre is the official name, and then to the York Minster."

"What's a Minster?" Ashlynn asked.

"A big church," I said.

"Not another church!" Katie complained.

"Yes, another church," I said.

We rode the bus until it stopped at Piccadilly. It was just a five--minute walk to the centre and museum. I had bought entrance tickets, so we only had to wait a half hour.

It fascinated the granddaughters that we got to ride carriages through the centre to view the exhibits. There was a commentary we could listen to as we looked at the depictions of what life was like in a 900 A. D. Viking village that was named Jorvik.

The experience as we traveled in the carriage was so real to the Viking time. Sights, sounds, and even smells enveloped our senses. The centre was built where part of the ancient village existed a thousand years before. Excavations by archaeologists had revealed artifacts of the time. The reconstructed houses, workshops, and backyards of the Viking age were done to perfection. We were there only a little over an hour, but it was an enlightening time.

When we exited, I turned to Sara and the girls and pointed toward York Minster. "I want to go there partly because many of the Archbishops of York who were the heads of the church here lived at Cawood Castle. One of them was responsible for building the Gatehouse where we're staying."

"Who was that?" Sara asked.

"John Kemp. He built it around 1426."

"You mean that room where I'm sleeping was built about six hundred years ago?" Katie asked.

"Yes. They've added electricity, running water, the bathrooms and kitchen since then. But that spiral staircase is ancient," I said.

When we arrived at the door to the Minster, I was excited. This was where at least seven of the Archbishops of York who lived at Cawood Castle were buried. There were probably more, but I had a list of six who lived and died at the castle and then were buried at York Minster.

We were met just inside with the decision to buy the ticket for the main tour or to purchase one that allowed us to walk up the staircase to the top of the tower. It was two hundred seventy-five steps to the top so that made my decision very easy. I was interested in the architecture and history, but I mainly wanted to see the burial crypt of the archbishops.

However, the girls wanted to walk to the top of the tower. They were over eight years of age, so they could go. There was always a volunteer tour guide who ascended the steps with every group.

"I think that will be exciting to look at the city from the top," Katie said. "More exciting than walking through this big church."

So, I purchased tickets for them to go to the top. "Now when you come back down, don't go out. Wait around this area for your grandmother and me." With that admonition, they were on their way to get in the queue to go up the spiral staircase.

The cathedral was huge—much larger than Selby Abbey. It dated from 1220 and before. Of course, it took hundreds of years to build and rebuild. Invasions, decay, and fire all had taken a toll on the magnificent structure at one time or another. It came to be known through digging and reconstruction that part of the building stood where a Roman fort had been maintained in the 200s.

When I got to the crypt area where many archbishops were buried, I took a list from my pocket to see if I could identify the ones who had died at Cawood Castle. William Greenfield had died in 1315; William Melton in 1340; William Zouche in 1352; John Thoresby in 1373; Thomas Rotherham in 1500; and Thomas Savage in 1507. Strangely, the crypt where Thomas Savage was buried was the only one I could identify. Our tour guide wasn't able to point out the other burial sites, either. I would have to ask Servant to bring them all to the Gatehouse for a meeting at some later date.

We spent a couple of hours looking at all the exhibits and viewing the windows and architecture of the Minster. It was evident that many religious people had invested a substantial amount of money and time in building, rebuilding, and maintaining the

Minster. With what was required to keep it up on a daily basis, I didn't regret the fee they charged for the tour or for the girls climbing to the top. I remembered the old saying that in England the churches charge for entry and the museums are free. At least that was the way it was in London.

The girls were waiting for us near the exit. "Wow, we really liked that view from the top," Katie said. "You could see the whole city. We saw the wall around the town. I want to go and walk that next."

I looked at my phone for the time. "Not today. We need to eat a late lunch and catch the bus back to the castle. You can come back another day to walk the wall." Katie and Ashlynn frowned their disappointment. They had a lot more energy than I had. At least I was noticing that they were not on their phones and electronic games as much now. They were becoming interested in the sights, sounds, and history of the area.

We arrived back at the Gatehouse a couple of hours before dark. We walked to the Pickled Postie to get a few necessities and another bundle of firewood. Although I was scheduled to meet Servant and the three kings on the roof of the gatehouse, it might be a good idea to have a fire for a few hours. I was still working on having Sara's approval for my trip to the roof at 3 A. M.

Later, we all ate sandwiches for our dinner. The girls headed upstairs to their room. I started the fire. Sara and I sat in the chairs with our feet up.

"Are you really planning to go up on the roof in the middle of the night?" Sara asked.

"Trust me. I will be safe. It will probably only take an hour to talk to all three kings. Servant will be there, too."

Sara shook her head. "I can't believe you think you're actually meeting with ghosts—or spirits."

"I wish I could prove it to you. But I don't know how. They're not bringing any trinkets for me to keep."

Sara stared at the fire. I could tell she wasn't convinced.

"I want you to wake me when you go up. I'll stay awake the hour that you're gone to be sure you come back down safely. And please don't wake the girls as you pass by."

That was as close to an agreement as I was going to get.

I set my alarm for fifteen until three, and we went to bed.

The vibration of my phone woke me at the appointed time. I rolled over and whispered to Sara, "I'm going up."

"Be careful and come down as soon as you can."

I put on a pair of soft slippers and made my way to our door and onto the staircase. I passed the bathroom a few steps up and then stepped softly by the door to the girls' room. A few more footfalls on the stone steps led me to the door to get to the roof. Earlier, I had set five chairs in a circle in the middle of the roof. Three kings, Servant, and I made five. I looked up. It was a beautiful star-lit night. The moon hung over the western wall. It was cool but not cold.

I chose a chair and sat anxiously waiting for my visitors. Suddenly to my left, Servant appeared in all his golden radiance sitting next to me.

"Are the others coming?" I asked him in my thoughts.

"Yes. I have been scurrying hither and yon to arrange this. To Scotland and back," I heard his answer. "They'll be here in a few minutes. How was your trip to York?"

"We enjoyed it a lot. The Jorvik Centre and the Minster were both more than advertised." I looked at Servant. "Servant, do you mind if I ask you something while we're waiting on the three kings?"

"No. Go ahead."

"You died physically about five hundred years ago. After you died, did the Great Spirit judge you?"

"No. People get that confused. There will be a big judgment day when the Great Spirit sends his Son back. Until then, our spirits have a chance to wander around. We may go through what you call in your judicial system a preliminary hearing. We might can guess our final destination, but we won't know for sure until then."

"Is it like Purgatory?" I asked.

"No. The Great Spirit sends some like George Neville to do penance but not all of us. He sent King Henry VIII to your America for a hundred years from 1690 until 1790 to see how things were where the citizens didn't want a king and wanted a division between church and state. We didn't have much of that here."

With that explanation from Servant, the other three chairs suddenly filled with the kings. They each appeared to be wearing radiant robes of different colors—one royal purple, one red, and one green.

When I looked at each one in turn, I thought they were most likely sitting in order of their birth or age. Henry III, I believed, was wearing the royal purple robe. Next to him was his son, Edward I, known as Longshanks for his height and length of his legs. He did appear to be about a foot taller than his father. He was adorned in a red fluorescent robe. I imagined that was symbolic of his warring nature. To his left was the one I believed to be Edward II, grandson of Henry and son of Edward I. He wore a robe as green as the early spring grass.

I heard loud chattering as they all seemed to talk at once. I looked at Servant and asked him in my thoughts, "Can you ask them to talk one at a time? I cannot decipher all the talk as it is running together."

Servant stood and went in front of each of them and spoke to them silently in however spirits talk to each other. The noise died down. Servant turned to me. "You can speak to them one at a time. They will listen and answer."

I reached into the only pocket I had and withdrew a paper with some notes and questions for each king. I would start with the oldest—Henry III.

"Your highness," I said in my thoughts, "I am happy you came back to Cawood Castle or what is left of it."

"Just call me Henry." I heard his voice. "I am happy to be here and meet a descendant of the original Cawood family."

"Thank you, Henry," I said. "My notes say that you became a king when you were only nine years old. Is that right?"

"Yes. Not much of a king at first. The older lords and barons and knights wanted to run things. They didn't believe a nine-year-old could be a powerful king. Sir William Marshall served as my protector. He was quite able militarily and defeated the rebels at the Battle of Lincoln.

"You know I reissued the Magna Carta in 1225.

"That was the forbearer of much of modern government, including your Constitution."

"I see," I said. He had lived and known a lot of history. "You were born in 1207 and became king in 1216. Your physical body lived until 1272—sixty-five years old?"

"Yes. That was pretty old for that day and time."

"You visited the castle in 1255. Is that correct?"

"Yes. It wasn't really much of a castle then—more like a large manor turning into a palace. This gatehouse where we're meeting wasn't here then. There were more wood walls with some stone."

"Why did you come here?" I asked.

"Two main reasons. I was very interested in building beautiful castles throughout the realm. Cawood Manor, Palace, or Castle was one that could be a beautiful place in this part of Yorkshire with a bit of care, money, and oversight."

"And what was the other reason?"

"To hunt the deer, my good man! This was an excellent hunting area. Your family were the keepers of the king's forests in this area, and they did an excellent job. Abundance of deer and some wild hogs. I was just forty-eight when I visited. I rode the horses and hunted the deer. A great holiday for a king."

"How did you do with foreign affairs?" I asked.

"That's still a sore point. You know they stole my ancestral lands in France. I could never get them back. And those Scots were always a sore lot. I had my troubles with them, but Edward here—the Hammer of the Scots--had almost continual war. And his son here—Edward II—continued fighting. His son, Edward the Third, had to make peace with Robert the Bruce.

"Like I said, I enjoyed building and rebuilding castles. During my reign, Westminster Abbey was rebuilt. I count that as one of my great accomplishments. There were many battles. I was captured one time, but my son here, Edward I, came to my rescue."

I looked at my phone for the time. I had promised Sara that I would be back down in about an hour. I didn't want her to worry. I had more to ask Henry, but I decided to move on to Edward I.

"King Edward," I thought and looked straight at him. I knew he was a warrior. It had been written that he was temperamental, that he was intimidating, and that he instilled fear in people. I didn't want to offend him. I didn't think spirits could toss me off the roof, but didn't want to risk it.

He answered in a soft voice. "You may call me Edward the First, not to be confused with my son here, Edward the Second, or my grandson, Edward the Third."

"Thank you. My research says you were born in 1239 and lived in your physical body until 1307. You became king in 1272. Is that right?"

"Yes. I was away on the Ninth Crusade to the Holy Land and returning when I learned of my father's death. And became king then. I had worked with my father before going on the crusade. There were battles we both fought in. I was captured one time, but I escaped shortly."

"You were quite a warrior, weren't you?"

"Not to brag. But I led our soldiers into battle. Kings were expected to lead and to go into battle during wars themselves. It wasn't like today where the leaders send the young men into war and sit on the sidelines to see what happens."

"Why did you go on the Ninth Crusade?"

"I wasn't king yet. And I knew the French King needed help. I took a force of about one thousand with a couple of hundred knights. We set sail. We had some good success against the Muslims. But they were a hearty fighting bunch. I stayed a little over a year, around 1270 and 1271. Then I headed back."

I looked around the gatehouse and back at Edward the First. "What is your connection with the Cawood Castle?"

"This was my home away from home for about seven years. I was fighting those dang Scots. When I needed a rest, I came back here. It wasn't that far from Scotland.

"You must know that I defeated William Wallace's forces at the Battle of Falkirk in 1298. That pretty well put down those rebellious Scots."

"You didn't capture Wallace at that time, did you?"

"No. He escaped. But seven years later, the traitor was captured."

"And you had him executed in London?"

"Yes, a traitor's death."

I didn't want to get him stirred up, so I turned to a more peaceful subject.

"My ancestor, David Cawood, who had been Abbot of Selby Abbey, petitioned you in 1302 for the return of some ancestral land."

"Yes. David was a good man. I couldn't do everything he wanted. But I restored some property to his family that the Archbishops of York had taken."

"Thank you. That's probably part of the property at Keesbury." I turned to another subject. "Where are you staying now?"

"Ha, ha. The Great Spirit has sent me to Scotland. I've been there for seven hundred years. Those Scots are a rather nice bunch now. I hang around where William Wallace lived. I guess it's my penance."

"Which nickname do you prefer—Longshanks or Hammer of the Scots?"

"I had several names like that, but Hammer of the Scots would be my preferred."

I looked at my phone again. My hour was running out. I turned toward Edward the Second.

"My research says you brought your wife, Queen Isabella, here in 1314."

"Yes, those were more peaceful times for me, except for Robert de Bruce. We were in between battles with the Scots. I was just thirty years old when I came here. I didn't become king until 1307. I was a fairly young king, just twenty-three. Isabella was still a faithful wife until she turned against me. Can't trust those French women."

"What happened to you? When you were deposed?"

"The barons and other aristocrats didn't like me. They spread rumors about my sexuality. They finally took me prisoner—and murdered me at Berkeley Castle in 1327. I was just forty-three years old.

"I did some good things and some bad. I must admit the bad while claiming the good. Letting Isabella go back to France was a mistake."

I looked at Servant who was shaking his head. I moved on to a more pleasant subject.

"What did you think of the Cawood Castle when you visited?"

"It wasn't much of a castle then. More like a manor or palace. Not walled in. No gatehouse. It was a very good hunting lodge, though."

I decided to end this visit with the three kings and go back downstairs.

"Thank you for coming. It was very enlightening to see you three from the same family as kings." I looked again at Servant. He stood and went in front of the other guests. It appeared he waved his hand. In an instant, the three were gone.

Servant turned toward me. "Who is next?" he asked.

"Any luck with Henry VIII or Thomas Wolsey?"

"Not yet. Henry is a piece of work, as you would say. I haven't talked with Wolsey."

"How about the seven archbishops of York who lived and died here at the castle?"

"I can do that. They are all at York or at All Saints' Church. Same time tomorrow. Here on the roof."

With that said, Servant disappeared. I went back downstairs to bed.

"Did you see your three kings?" Sara asked.

"Yes. A very nice visit."

"Sure," she said and turned over.

Chapter Six

A Convocation of Archbishops

A few hours later Sara and I awoke to the sound of the girls running down the stairs.

"Where are we going today?" Katie asked.

"I don't know," I said. "We may just walk around the village here or go into Selby. Just have a relaxing day."

"I still want to walk the walls in York," Katie said.

"And I want to see the animals in the Garth," Ashlynn responded.

"We can go to York tomorrow. Why don't you girls go into the kitchen and fix breakfast for your grandparents?" I asked.

With that said they turned and walked toward the kitchen. Sara and I slowly rolled out of bed and went to the table to await whatever the girls decided to cook for breakfast.

"So, you had a nice visit with your three kings?" Sara asked.

"Yes. You won't believe it. There was a father, son, and grandson. All had been kings of England. And all three had visited here in the 1200s and 1300s."

"Did you learn anything?"

"Yes. I learned not to doubt the ability of Servant to bring the spirits back to the castle."

"Oh, yes. Servant. How was he?"

"Fine. He asked about our trip to York."

Sara nodded her head. Katie brought us each a glass of orange juice.

"I'll go and make us some coffee," I said and got up to walk to the kitchen.

When I came back to the table, I decided to ask Sara if we could stay longer at the castle if it was available. I was unsure if I could see and talk with all the old spirits in the time we had left on our reservation.

"Are you going to see any other ghosts tonight?" Sara asked.

"Well, you're probably not going to believe this, but I asked Servant to invite the seven Archbishops of York who lived and six died here to come for a visit on the roof tonight."

"Oh, seven plus you and Servant. Do you think the roof will accommodate all of you? Sounds like it will be a noisy place."

"As I said before, there is no actual noise or sound. We can only hear each other and communicate in silence through mental telepathy."

"I forgot," Sara said and rolled her eyes.

"I wanted to ask you if you would be OK with staying an extra week here. I really want to see Thomas Wolsey and King Henry VIII?"

"An extra week? Is the gatehouse available? We only booked a week. What about the girls?"

"I'll bribe them with trips to the outlet mall. They can walk the York walls and do other things. I would have to check with Landmark Trust to see if it's available."

"OK. One more week. And then we'll go home. If you promise to see a psychiatrist when we get back to Tennessee."

"A deal," I said and smiled.

The girls fixed my favorites—bacon and eggs for breakfast. Sara had a fruit bowl and some toast.

"I'm going to walk down to the Pickled Postie and get a few things. Then we'll walk around the village or go to Selby," I said.

"Can we go with you?" Katie and Ashlynn asked at the same time.

"Sure. That will give your grandmother time to get ready."

We were down the stairs and out the door while Sara finished her cup of coffee.

At the Pickled Postie, I picked out a few food items to take back to the castle. Standing in line to pay, I noticed the gentleman I had met before ahead of me.

"Good day, John. How are you?"

He turned and smiled. "Oh, Chris. I'm fine. How are you? Enjoying your stay at the gatehouse?"

"Yes. We've been to York. Saw the Minster and the Jorvik Centre. We're thinking about going back to Selby today."

"What a coincidence. I'm going in a bit. Why don't you ride with me, and I'll show you around? There are you and your wife and these two girls, right?"

"Yes. That's very kind of you."

"We're only supposed to have no more than four people in our vehicle, but I believe these two young ladies could squeeze together and count as one."

In a few minutes John was picking us up in front of the castle fence. He was such an informative fellow. He had served on the local council for several years. He told us a lot about the area on our drive.

"Would you like to see the municipal building? There's a plaque in one of the rooms with one of your distant relative's names inscribed on it."

John's tour of the town was quite informative. The visit to the municipal building was a treat to see "A. Cawood" listed on the plaque as a former council person.

We drove through the narrow streets of Selby, going by the train station, and circling by the Abbey. At lunch time, John suggested we go to Mister C's just a block or so from the Abbey. It did not disappoint. I had fish and chips. The girls got hamburgers. Sara tried a chicken salad. Just about everyone at Mister C's knew John. I thought he was a local celebrity, but he denied it.

By the time we arrived back at the castle, it was late afternoon. "Thank you for your kindness," I told John. "Maybe we'll see you again. We've decided to add a week to our holiday if the gatehouse is available."

"Oh, that would be splendid. If you need anything, ring me up. I live directly across the street."

As soon as we walked up the stairs, the girls headed to their room to rest. I took my phone and looked for Landmark Trust's site. When I found it, we lucked out. The gatehouse was available for another week. So, all together I would have another ten days and nights to visit with the spirits that Servant would bring.

At dinner time we walked to the Castle Inn. We decided it was the best and nearest place in walking distance for good food. We had not yet tried the Jolly Sailor or the Ferry Inn for meals since we didn't know whether the girls could go to a pub or if they served meals.

It was dark by the time we arrived back at the castle. The girls went up to their room. I sat down and tried to do a bit more research on the archbishops I was going to meet in the wee hours of the morning.

"Is your rendezvous for 3 a. m again?" Sara asked.

"Yes."

"Well, let me know when you go up and come back down. And be very careful. Don't wander around and fall off the roof."

At the appointed time, I rolled out of the bed and made my quiet trek up the stone stairway. The five chairs were still on the roof. I left them in the same positions they were in the night before. There were two where Servant and I sat, and three were a few feet away facing the other two. With seven guests expected, there wouldn't be enough chairs to accommodate them all. They could stand. I didn't think they would mind standing—or hovering—or whatever spirits do.

I sat down and waited for Servant. Among all his qualities, Servant had always been punctual. He was this time also. I turned to my left, and there he was in the chair next to me. He seemed to be sparkling or glistening more than usual.

"I wanted to look sharp for the seven archbishops who will be visiting," I heard Servant say in my head.

"Are they all coming?" I asked.

"Yes. Six from their burial crypts at York Minster, and George 'Big Mountain' Montaigne is coming up the short distance from All Saints Church here in Cawood."

I rubbed my hands together in excitement and anticipation. I took the paper I had from my pocket with notes about each archbishop.

At first, I thought it was a lightning strike when I saw a flash of brilliant colorful light. But it landed behind the three chairs. It wasn't lightning, but it was more like a rainbow settling on the roof. Then I could see them—seven figures adorned in robes the seven colors of the rainbow. Their heads appeared coned shape, but their robes left no doubt as to their importance.

I gazed and counted. From left to right they wore robes of red, orange, yellow, green, blue, indigo, and violet. They all appeared to be standing and aligned perfectly behind the three chairs. Then I heard their voices mingling like a cacophony of crickets and frogs in a bog. I couldn't understand a word that was being said.

I turned to Servant. "Ask them to speak one at a time so I can understand."

Servant alighted and went in front of them. He told them words I couldn't hear, but they quieted.

"Servant, I want to talk with them one at a time in the order of when they lived at the castle. If each could come at his time and sit or stand or hover in front of the middle chair. I would like to start with William Greenfield."

Servant turned toward me, and I heard him say, "That is the way they are lined up. Greenfield is in the red robe on one end and Montaigne is on the other end in the violet robe." Servant then turned back toward the group. I thought I saw him motion for Greenfield to come to the middle of the three chairs.

I looked at my phone to get the time. I had promised Sara I would be back down in about an hour. That would give me no more than eight minutes each with the seven archbishops.

The red-robed Archbishop Greenfield came and sat in the middle chair. I could tell that he was a man with much dignity. What appeared to be his eyes stared directly at me.

"Archbishop Greenfield, glad you could come."

"I was happy to come. So many tourists traipsing around York Minster that I enjoy getting away. I especially like coming back to Cawood where I lived in what was a palace then. And, of course, I died physically here in 1315."

"You had an extraordinary life. You studied at Oxford. Then you went to Paris for more studies and became a doctor in civil and canon law," I said in my mind.

"I enjoyed the study of law. It helped me in my role as Lord Chancellor. Servant told me you are a lawyer in America. Is that right?"

"Yes. I am mainly retired now. After Paris, did you go somewhere else in Europe?"

"Yes, then I went to Rome and became indebted for my living expenses. When I came back to England, my friend, King Edward the First, appointed me Lord Chancellor in 1302, and I controlled the Great Seal. I wasn't installed as archbishop until 1306."

"How did you get to be Archbishop of York?" I asked.

"My connections, my Dear Man. I had lived in Rome and knew the Pope and people around him. I was Lord Chancellor, so I was in with the king. Edward recommended me, and the Pope agreed. Back then we were Catholic. That was before Henry VIII broke away.

"All of the appointments to be archbishop involved both political and religious clout. You had to have the recommendation of the king for the Pope to go along."

"King Edward the First was here last night with his father and son," I said.

"Yes. That whole family of kings were very accommodating chaps. The Hammer of the Scots was especially kind to me."

"Why did you choose to live at what was then Cawood Palace?"

"Several reasons. First, it was nicer than anything in York. York had become the de facto capital of England because of the wars with the Scots and there were many political and court people trying to find places to live. Secondly, the palace was on the south side of the River Ouse protecting us from the invasive Scots. Lastly, I could come and go to the York Minster without too long a trip."

"You died here at the Palace in 1315. And you were buried at York Minster?"

"Yes. York Minster is a lovely place. Before me and after me, about every archbishop chose to be buried there. Except for Big Mountain over there," he said and motioned toward the end of the line where George Montaigne stood in his violet robe.

I decided to move on to the next archbishop. "Thank you, Archbishop Greenfield." I turned to Servant and indicated I needed Archbishop William Melton to come forward.

Archbishop William Melton moved around to the front in his bright orange robe and sat down in the middle chair.

"Sir, thank you for coming," I said.

"This is a fine group of men you have here. I heard you talking about King Edward the First. His son, King Edward the Second was kind to me. I was appointed Controller of the Wardrobe when he became king."

"You held several positions."

"I was the Lord Treasurer during 1325 and 1326. That was also part of the time I was Archbishop of York. I served from 1317 until my physical death in 1340."

"You not only were a religious figure in being archbishop, but you also were politically and militarily a leader."

"Those Scots made raids into York destroying churches and sacking monasteries. They were a terrible lot."

"You led a group of citizen soldiers against the Scots in 1319."

"Yes, that didn't turn out well. King Edward the Second's wife, Isabella had to flee York and go to Nottingham."

"You had some trouble with the nuns and especially Joan of Leeds, didn't you?" I asked.

"Yes. I don't know which ones were more fierce—those Scots or the nuns. You've done your research."

"On the positive side, you built the Nave at York Minster."

"Not me, personally. But I had it built."

"Did you enjoy your time here at what was then Cawood Palace?"

"Yes. It was a wonderful place to live. Lovely people and a lovely village. I stayed until I died physically in 1340. My body was buried in York Minster in the north aisle of the nave."

I began to see a pattern with the archbishops. They all seemed to have risen through the ranks of working for royalty, and the kings, in particular, until they came to their positions as archbishops. There they stayed until they died. They all seemed to be highly educated, going to universities in England and France. They were in well with the popes of their times.

Besides being ecclesiastical leaders, it seems that most were also involved in civil government. Some even led soldiers in battle-especially against the Scots.

My hour was running swiftly along. I had to move on to the next archbishop if I was to finish on time. I looked over to Servant. He understood and moved toward the row of archbishops.

Archbishop William Zouche in his brilliant yellow robe came around and sat in the middle chair. I looked at my notes. He lived from 1290 until 1352 when he died at Cawood Castle.

"Thank you also for coming, Archbishop Zouche. How do you like the roof of the gatehouse?"

"Very nice. The sparkling stars are lovely. And what is even more lovely is to be here with all my Brother Archbishops. The gatehouse wasn't here when I lived at the palace. It is a great addition. We all lived at Cawood Palace or what became Cawood Castle. And all of us except for Big Mountain died here. Six of us are buried at York Minster. Big Mountain chose to be buried here in the village at All Saints Church."

"You also studied Canon Law at Oxford."

"Very useful in my position as archbishop."

"How did you become archbishop?" I asked.

"It wasn't easy. I was early on the Keeper of the Wardrobe for the king's house. That entailed more than looking after clothing. I oversaw all expenses and all revenue coming in. In 1337 I was promoted to Lord Treasurer—again responsible for money and expenditures."

"I read that King Edward the Third wanted someone else to be Archbishop of York," I said.

"Yes, the king and I had a little tiff. The leaders of the church in York—they called them Canons of York—elected me in 1340. But because of the king's reluctance, I wasn't consecrated until 1342. Pope Clement the Sixth took care of that."

"But you got back into the good graces of King Edward the Third."

"It took a victory in battle against the Scots to do it. I led troops into the Battle of Neville's Cross in October 1346. I saved the king's reputation."

"Did you have any other hard times while archbishop?"

"The Black Death was spreading across England and Europe. So many people died of it that I was afraid to bury them in our normal cemeteries. I asked and got permission from the Pope to open new cemeteries just for those who died of the Black Death."

"It must have been a horrible time."

"We didn't know at that time how it was spread and had very few remedies for it. I stayed away from it the best I could by remaining at the palace for a long time."

"Thank you for coming." I looked at my phone for the time. I had to move on quickly. The next archbishop would be John Thoresby. I looked at the row of archbishops. He was wearing a green robe glistening like grass in the morning dew.

I stared at my notes. The first three archbishops had lived at Cawood Palace, later to be Cawood Castle, for about fifty years in the early to mid-1300s. I knew the castle belonged to and was occupied by the Archbishops of York for around two hundred years. In my quest for my ancestors and their places of abode, I was learning a lot of local history from the ghosts of Cawood Castle—or as they preferred—the Spirits of Cawood Castle. Who would believe me, though? I had to write down all my encounters even if they were just for my information.

I moved along to John Thoresby. He had served a considerable time as archbishop—from 1354 to 1373. He came around and took the middle chair as had the previous ones. I was pleasantly surprised that they all seemed so cordial. Then I considered that most of them had been physically dead for nearly seven hundred years. It might be that their spirits longed for some interaction and recognition by those living physically now.

"You were born in Yorkshire?" I asked.

"Yes, in Thoresby. That's how I got my surname—John of Thoresby. It was the same with your ancestors—John De Cawood—wasn't it?"

"Yes." I was a bit surprised that he knew my ancestral history. "You served King Edward the Third in several capacities?"

"Among other offices I was the Lord Keeper of the Privy Seal. That was the king's personal seal."

"The Pope also favored you?"

"Pope Clement the Sixth appointed me Bishop of Saint David's. I was selected as Lord Chancellor of England in 1349."

"You had no trouble being appointed as Archbishop of York?"

"No. My appointment was unanimous and approved by both the king and Pope."

"Did you have any problems in being archbishop?"

"Quite a few at the beginning. The highest offices in York Minster were in the hands of the Roman Cardinals who, of course, were non-residents of York. I issued my catechism right here from Cawood Palace in 1373. That settled some issues. Then there were the differences between the Archbishops of Canterbury and those of York. They were worked out during my time of service."

"What did you think of Cawood Palace?"

"It was absolutely the best residence for the Archbishops of York. I started a renewed building program at York Minster, but Cawood Palace was ideal for living day by day."

"You died here at the palace?"

"Yes. I died here in November 1373. I had prepared a place for my physical body to be buried at York Minster before the altar of the Virgin in the Lady Chapel which I had constructed."

There was much more that each of these archbishops had done during their lives. I was sure they would want to recount those events, but my time for interviewing was running out.

"Thank you, Archbishop Thoresby, for coming. I need to move on to Archbishop Thomas Rotherham."

Rotherham was adorned in a royal blue robe. He was moving to the middle chair as Thoresby was turning to go back to his place in line. Rotherham had served a hundred years after Thoresby—from 1480 to 1500. He had died at Cawood Castle of the Plague.

I was interested at this time only in the archbishops who had lived at Cawood Palace or Castle and who had died here. Big Mountain Montaigne had lived here but died in London. I knew several others had lived here but died at other places too. Rotherham, having died of the Plague, would be interesting.

When I scanned my notes on the archbishops, I saw similarities in their rise to the position of Archbishop of York. They all seemed to be highly educated. Also, they rose through the ranks of service to their kings. They all appeared to be well connected not only to the royalty of the time but to the religious leaders, including the popes.

"Archbishop Rotherham, thank you for coming. How was it that you and your brothers here all rose to become Archbishops of York?"

He appeared to turn and look at each of the others in line behind him.

"I believe we all came from wealthy families. We were able to get the best education at the best universities of the day. Our families had connections with the kings of the day and the religious higher ups.

"We were privileged people. With our wealth and influential families, we were able to receive appointments from our kings. Money bought influence. Money bought privilege. And once we got into the king's favor, we could move up the ladder to where our final appointment would be to serve as Archbishops of York."

I nodded my head. Politics had not changed much over the past six hundred years. Rotherham had been the Keeper of the Privy Seal under King Edward the Fourth. He had also served as Ambassador to France and then to Burgundy.

"You had a bit of a problem with the politics of the day at one time, didn't you?"

"Yes. I was dismissed as Lord Chancellor. I favored dowager queen Elizabeth Woodville in her attempt to have control of the young new king, Edward the fifth. I was imprisoned in the Tower of London for a month. But I didn't go to the chopping block. Then I regained favor and returned to my position at York."

"You didn't physically die until 1500 at age seventy-six. But I read that you died of the plague. Is that correct?"

"Yes. There were several outbreaks of the plague, or Black Death. I was fortunate to live as long as I did. They didn't know what to do with the bodies of those who died of the plague. They were afraid of the contamination and spread of disease from dead bodies. I died in 1500 but my body was not buried in York Minster for five years."

I decided to test his knowledge of world history.

"You lived for eight years after Christopher Columbus' voyage to the 'New World'. Did you know of that event in your lifetime?"

"Yes. The so-called Dark Ages were over. We had communication with Spain and other countries. Generally, we didn't think much would come of his voyages and discoveries. It took us until the late 1500s and early 1600s before we had people to go there. Some were successful and some not so much. At least I understand you have a New York named for our old York."

I looked at Servant. It was almost time to end these talks, and I still had two more to go.

"Yes, New York is a great city, but I do like the York here just a few miles up the road. Thank you for coming."

Servant was already up and moving toward Archbishop Thomas Savage in the indigo robe. My notes said savage lived from 1449 until 1507 when he died here at the castle. He was archbishop from 1501 to 1507.

"Thank you for coming, Archbishop Savage. The Cawood Palace had grown into Cawood Castle by the time you lived here?"

"Yes. As the others have said, it was a lovely place. A lot of important folks lived or visited here. They were still talking forty years later about the feast that George Neville gave."

"Quite a big deal," I said. "He was here a couple of days ago. Spends most of his time in London now. Your family was in good with King Henry VII, weren't you?"

"Yes, my brother, John Savage, had been one of the King's commanders at the Battle of Bosworth Field. That victory put Henry on the throne. Henry was the first king of the Tudor dynasty. I might say that victory achieved for my family great prominence and privilege."

"Like most of the others here, you served the king as ambassador?"

"Yes. Ambassador to Castille and Portugal. I loved those assignments at those lovely countries."

"You had an important role for the king here in Yorkshire."

"King Henry appointed me as commissioner and leader of the Council of the North. Henry Percy, Earl of Northumberland, caused me a lot of trouble. Thirteen of his armed riders came through Fulford where I had just passed with eighty armed riders. He should have known that he was outnumbered. No one died but there was a bit of a standoff and a lot of shouting and waving of swords. Afterwards, the king summoned both me and the Earl to London. The king fined both of us two thousand pounds.

"I thought it was unjust. My career faltered after that. I died here three years later. My earthly body was buried at York Minster."

"You had quite a career. Thanks for coming."

Servant was already up proceeding to the last archbishop in line—George Montaigne—who was locally known as Big Mountain. Clad in his violet robe, he came around to the middle chair.

"Archbishop, happy you could join us."

"Ha, ha, it is not far from All Saints Church here in Cawood where my body is buried."

"Yes, I wanted to ask you about that. Why the church here in the village rather than York Minster?"

"I thought it was the proper thing to do. I was born here and grew up here. I even knew some of your Cawood ancestors. The Castle had been refurbished by Cardinal Wolsey in 1529 but had deteriorated again by the time I lived here.

"I only was Archbishop of York for about four months before my death. I didn't think so short a service allowed me to be buried with archbishops who had served many years. Besides, All Saints Church was my church in my youth."

"By the time you served, the religion had changed from Catholic to Church of England?"

"Yes, thanks to King Henry the Eighth and his dalliances. I might say Henry knew where the money was--in the churches and monasteries."

"You are noted for making a statement to King Charles I."

"Ha, ha, I don't know whether I really said it, but it sounds like something I would say. 'Hadst thou faith as a grain of mustard seed, thou would say unto this mountain be removed into that sea.' I was generally quoting from Matthew 17:20. But the mountain was me—Montaigne—and the sea was the see of York. Whatever I said, it worked. My appointment came and my death just a short time later. I died in London with instructions to bury me at All Saints Church."

"A beautiful church," I said.

I looked once again at my phone. I had gone for over an hour. Sara would be worried about me. It was time to go. I was moved by what Montaigne had said. He was a humble man who was born and buried in Cawood. He knew where his roots were. He had travelled a lot and served the king and church, but he came home in the end.

"Thank you all for coming. It's time to go for now. Maybe we can all get together again."

The line of archbishops started turning toward each other and speaking in chattering voices I could hear again as I did at the beginning.

I turned to Servant. "Do we need to tell them to go?"

"No" Servant said. "They will go when they finish talking with each other."

Just then I felt a drop of rain hit my hand. I looked up. The stars had disappeared above a canopy of clouds. More drops came. I looked back to the glistening robes of the archbishops as the rain became heavier. The robes and archbishops disappeared into the darkness.

Chapter Seven

John Kemp

The rain continued throughout the night. Sara did not awaken when I came back to bed half an hour later than expected. Servant and I had talked after the seven archbishops had left. Who would he bring next? I suggested Cardinal Wolsey or King Henry the Eighth.

Servant shook his head. "Not yet. Henry is recalcitrant and Wolsey is away. But I have contacted John Kemp. He's agreeable. You remember that he had the gatehouse built in 1426?"

"Yes. He would be fine."

The rain drops pattered against the windows but did not stop us from sleeping in for another hour. The granddaughters even stayed quietly upstairs for longer than usual.

When we did get up, I went first to the kitchen to make coffee. Sara stayed in bed until I brought the coffee and some toast to the table.

"Where are we going or what are we going to do today?" Sara asked.

I looked out the window. It was a steady rain that showed no signs of letting up. "We may just stay in today. Relax, read, talk, and go back to York tomorrow."

"What about the girls? You think they will be fine with just hanging around?"

"We'll see," I said.

Sara finished her toast and then looked over at me. "How did your meeting go last night? It didn't rain on you and your guests, did it?"

I could hear her skepticism in the tone of her voice. "No. The rain started just as we concluded."

"Were they communicating by mental telepathy again?"

"Yes. It was noisy at the beginning because I could hear them all. I had to ask Servant to tell them to talk one at a time."

"Oh, yes. Servant. How is he?"

"Great. He's making all the arrangements."

"He must be in good with all the ghosts—or spirits."

"Yes, he is. He arranges things with the help of the Great Spirit."

"Is the Great Spirit the same as God?"

"I think so," I said.

"Did they all show up?"

"Yes. All seven. And you won't believe this—they were each dressed in a robe the colors of the rainbow. Seven colors in order—red, orange, yellow, green, blue, indigo, and violet."

Sara shook her head. "That was decent of them. Are you through with your meetings? Are there anymore?"

I took a bite of toast and a sip of coffee. "More," I said. "He's bringing John Kemp tonight—actually, early morning."

"Oh, won't you get wet if this rain doesn't stop?"

"We're meeting in front of the fireplace again," I said and pointed to the chairs near the fireplace.

"John Kemp? Isn't he the one you said built this gatehouse?"

"Yes. He was another Archbishop of York. He built the gatehouse in 1426 according to Servant. Some say it was 1445, but I'll take Servant's word for it."

"Nearly six hundred years ago. I'm sure he'll be proud of how it's lasted."

"Yes."

"You're still going to see the psychiatrist when we get home, aren't you? Talk with him about the apparitions and visions you're having?"

"I'll see him. But these spirits or ghosts are real. I wish I could prove it to you."

"Ask Servant to let me see and talk with him by 'mental telepathy.' Then I may believe."

"Do you believe in mental telepathy?" I asked.

Sara slowly shook her head. "Well, sometimes I can read your mind. Like when you want that last piece of chocolate pie. Or when you want me to be quiet while you're watching a ballgame."

"You believe in silent prayer, though, don't you? That's the Great Spirit or God reading your mind through mental telepathy."

"Yes, but that is God doing it."

"If God can do it, and we are creations of God, is it possible for us to do it?"

"Okay. But I thought you said your ghost or spirit friends didn't have bodies. If they don't have real bodies, how can they have brains?"

"I'm not sure. Their spirits have some means of communicating and movement. I don't guess I will know for sure until I join them."

"You mean when you die?"

"Yes."

"Do those ghosts have souls? Are souls different from spirits?" she asked.

"Good questions. I may have to ask Servant to see if he knows."

"Also, do your spirits haunt people or places?"

"So far, they all have been friendly. They only visit when they are invited."

"I thought you said Servant appeared the first night without invitation."

"Yes, he did. But that was because he had seen me at the Ferry Inn looking at the board about the Great Feast."

Thankfully for me, the girls ran down the stairs and into our room.

"What are we doing today?" Katie asked.

"It's raining. Maybe we can just stay here," I said.

"That's boring. How about we walk to the Pickled Postie and around the Garth?"

"Do you and Ashlynn have rain jackets?" I asked.

"Yes!" Ashlynn shouted.

They ran off and up the stairs to get their jackets.

"I think I'll stay here," Sara said. "You can walk with the girls."

With all three of us dressed in rain gear, the girls and I went downstairs, out the gatehouse door, and turned toward the street. Drops of rain blew against my face. I pulled my hooded jacket tighter. The girls seemed to delight in trotting in the rain and jumping over puddles.

We were able to get a table at the Pickled Postie without a reservation. The girls had gotten to know the waitress behind the counter in our short stay. They actually ordered a healthy cereal breakfast while I went for another order of bacon and eggs with coffee. There weren't as many people coming and going this time because of the rain. I overheard conversation about the bridge over the River Ouse being closed for part of the day for repairs.

After breakfast the girls wanted to walk up the street past the Jolly Sailor and loop around to where there was another entrance to the Castle Garth.

"Look at those ducks," Ashlynn said when we crossed the dyke. "There's at least eight of them."

The locals and Landmark Trust had been able to preserve several acres around the castle area as green land. It was an area where people could walk and enjoy the outdoors without the worry of autos nearby. Sometimes they allowed sheep to graze in the area, but we saw none on this day. It was also popular for an area to walk dogs. The rain had driven most dog walkers inside and we had the Garth nearly to ourselves. The rain didn't stop Katie and Ashlynn from walking, skipping, and running along the paths while I meandered at a much slower pace.

We ended our walk through the Garth at the rear and east end of the gatehouse and its attached brick banqueting hall.

"You should have gone with us, Nana," Ashlynn said to Sara when we got back to our room. "We had breakfast at the Pickled Postie and walked all through the Garth. There were ducks and other birds out there."

We shook off our wet rain gear into the corner near the kitchen. The girls turned toward me. "Bobo, are you sure there are no ghosts here? We thought we heard one last night," Katie said.

"That was probably me walking to the bathroom," I said. "If there are any ghosts here, I'll take care of them and protect you," I said and showed them a clinched fist. With that they ran off up the stairway.

We spent the remainder of the day lounging around and reading. I did as much research on John Kemp as I could on my phone with the weak internet signal we had at the gatehouse. We stayed in for our meals of sandwiches and soup. The girls said it was a lot like going camping. The rain continued into the night.

I started another fire when it got dark. Sara and I sat and read by lamplight and the glow of the fire.

Sara had relented to my appointed get together with Servant and John Kemp by the time we went to bed.

"Just tell me when your rendezvous is over," she said.

I was just as anxious for this meeting as for the others I had. I could barely close my eyes. Thoughts and questions ran through my mind. What would I ask John Kemp, and would he really come?

Fifteen minutes before the arranged time, I rolled out of bed, went to the kitchen to retrieve a bottle of water, and then went and sat in my chair near the fireplace. The wood had burned down to glowing red and orange embers.

Suddenly, Servant appeared in the chair nearest the kitchen leaving the middle chair for our guest.

"Is he coming?" I asked Servant in my thoughts.

"Yes. He will be here shortly."

"You didn't know him when you lived here, did you?"

"No. I was just a year old when he died, and he had been translated, or as you would say, 'transferred', to Canterbury before I was born."

There was no sound but just a rush of luminescent light when the middle chair filled with the spirit of John Kemp. His clothing, a robe again, was brighter than any of the seven archbishops I had met with the night before. I thought it was probably because Kemp had been archbishop of both York and Canterbury during his lifetime.

"Welcome, Archbishop Kemp," I said in my mind. I looked toward him hoping that he heard me.

It appeared as though he had. He turned his head toward me.

"I'm happy to be back," I heard him say. "This is a wondrously built gatehouse. It has survived with elegance for nearly six hundred years."

I looked at my notes. "You became Archbishop of York in 1426 and kept that position for twenty-six years. Is that correct?"

"Yes. Then I became Archbishop of Canterbury. But my physical body died at Canterbury just a short two years later in 1454. I was buried there at Canterbury in what you would call the choir loft, although it was not a loft at all. I lived to be seventy-four which was old for that day and time."

"In your years here as Archbishop of York, you lived here at the Cawood Palace or Castle?"

"Yes."

"Why did you build this beautiful gatehouse?"

I could see that the spirit of John Kemp moved as though he was looking around the room.

"It was needed. When I first went to York, I walked around the city. I walked on the walls and through the gatehouses there. They called them 'bars.' They could be closed to protect the city from intruders.

"Cawood Palace didn't have any fortified entrance at that time. I thought it necessary, in order to make it a true castle, to have a fortified gatehouse like those at York. It added protection and gave it a grander look. I started the gatehouse as soon as I was installed as archbishop, but it took quite a while to build—to build properly. It took almost twenty years.

"We had to get stone from the quarry. Most of it came up the Ouse and had to be unloaded and transported from the river to the castle. I had to get the best architects and stone masons. It was a massive undertaking. I felt much like the Pharaohs must have felt in building the pyramids.

"We didn't have the modern tools and appliances to lift the stone and set it in proper alignment. We didn't want it to be leaning like that tower over in Pisa, Italy. We had to use plumb bobs to do vertical and horizontal correctly. It took years, but it has withstood the test of time. Winds have blown, storms have come, and floods have risen, but here she stands. I consider it my finest accomplishment."

"It certainly has lasted a long time," I said. "They tore down most of the castle but left your gatehouse standing," I said.

I could see a change in color on Kemp's face area. He seemed angry, and his face glowed a bright red—redder than the wood embers in the fireplace.

"Those dastardly Roundheads of Parliament. They butchered King Charles and slighted several of the castles here in the north where the king had supporters. They tore down the tower over the gatehouse but left most of it. Of course, that was after my physical time, but I hovered over much of the action during that civil war."

I didn't want to anger the archbishop further, but I wanted to ask him about what someone had written about him.

"I read that someone said you were 'a politician first and hardly at all a bishop.' He said that you neglected the duties of being a religious bishop. What do you say to that?"

The color of his face returned to what it had been. He appeared to be calming down.

"That's close to true," he said. "I was a politician first. I was Lord Chancellor. I was Keeper of the Privy Seal. I was appointed Archbishop of York and then Archbishop of Canterbury. I was a very privileged person. Wealth buys privilege and privilege buys power and power gives more privilege. I was a politician first. I held the highest offices in the realm under the king.

"I left most of the religious duties to bishops and priests under me. Sometimes I wasn't careful enough to see that they carried out their duties."

I looked over at Servant who seemed to be motioning me to get back to nicer things.

"My family and I have certainly enjoyed staying at your gatehouse. It is a wonderful structure. Thanks for coming and thank you for building this magnificent building."

"Yes. I spent many years building it. And I sat right here on many a night enjoying the fireplace."

I looked over at Servant who nodded his approval. I was trying to dismiss archbishop John Kemp with kind words.

"Thank you for coming. I enjoyed reading about your illustrious career."

Servant nodded his head. It appeared he was whispering to the archbishop. In a few seconds, the spirit of the archbishop vanished.

"I have good news," Servant said.

"What?"

"Cardinal Thomas Wolsey has agreed to come tomorrow. On the roof if it's not raining."

"Oh, great. I'll have to get ready. You are a great friend, Servant."

Chapter Eight

Cardinal Thomas Wolsey

The rain had stopped by the time I woke up. I looked at my phone. This was Sunday. I immediately started thinking about what Servant had said. Thomas Wolsey was going to visit at the gatehouse roof in the early hours of the morning. Except for the kings who visited, he was the most famous.

No one was awake except for me. I went into the kitchen and made a pot of coffee. I had to be fully awake to plan and understand what this visit would mean. As soon as it had brewed, I took a large cup of coffee to the table near the window. The sun was casting its rays on the entrance to the gatehouse. It bathed the entire structure in a golden glow.

My mind flashed back to 1529 and 1530 when Wolsey lived here. He had been appointed Archbishop of York but seemingly never got to enjoy the position. I would have to review his history before our meeting.

When Sara awoke and the grandchildren came down from their room, we decided to have breakfast here at the gatehouse and then walk down to All Saints Church for the Sunday morning service. Ashlynn and Katie busied themselves with fixing breakfast for their grandparents.

I then told Sara about who was coming next.

"Thomas Wolsey? Wasn't he arrested here and taken off to London to be tried for treason?"

"Yes. He was arrested here, but he died on his way to London at Leicester. He was buried there at their abbey. But it's been destroyed, and his grave lost to history."

"And Servant is bringing him for a visit?"

"Yes."

"Oh, my," she said and shook her head.

With breakfast over, we dressed for church.

The walk to the church as a family was refreshing in the air of early May. The girls walked faster than we did. They would have to stop occasionally for us to catch up. It took us fifteen minutes to walk to the church. Two ladies greeted us at the door. After introductions, they seemed pleased and a bit excited that a Cawood family from America was visiting. I saw and spoke to the lady who had opened the door for me a few days before when I met with Servant and my ancestor, John Cawood, whose body was buried beneath the floor of the church.

With about thirty worshippers in attendance, there were plenty of empty pews for us to take our place. I had never been to a Church of England worship service before and didn't know exactly what to expect. But it was not so different from where we normally worshipped. There were hymns, scripture reading, and prayer.

When the vicar stood to deliver the sermon or homily, I looked over to a vacant pew to my left and in front. Suddenly, my friend, Servant, appeared. He glanced back at me. Then beside him came my ancestor, John Cawood, and Archbishop George Montaigne.

They all turned toward me for a few seconds before giving their full attention to the vicar.

I gently elbowed Sara and whispered, "Look, there are Servant, John Cawood, and Archbishop Montaigne on that pew in front and to our left."

Sara stared at the pew that I mentioned, but she said she saw nothing. Then I remembered only I could see the spirits. I had thought for a few seconds maybe they would appear to everyone there. But that was not to be.

Toward the end of the service, one parishioner invited us up to partake of the Holy Communion or Eucharist—or as we called it in our church at home—the Lord's Supper or Communion. Sara and I went forward and knelt. I thought it was kind of them to invite us to partake, and we did. I looked over to where my spirit friends had been seated. They stayed until the service was over and then vanished.

After the service, we stayed and talked with several people. Upon telling them a brief account of our family history, they all seemed to relish the idea of a Cawood coming to visit his ancestral village. I asked, but no one seemed to know where the graves beneath the floor were exactly. The stone floor had been covered with overlayments of carpet and tile. I thought to myself that I should have asked John Cawood to point out to me where the exact location of his grave was.

We walked to the Castle Inn for lunch. It was actually nearer than the gatehouse. Again, we were not disappointed with the offerings on the menu.

I had the battered mushrooms and onion rings for a starter, which I shared with Sara. I ordered the homemade Castle Pie for my main course while Sara took the stuffed chicken breast. Both granddaughters ordered chicken nuggets. For dessert we ordered two different ones--a chocolate brownie with ice cream and a slice of apple pie with vanilla ice cream. The girls settled for bowls of ice cream, with caramel topping on one and chocolate on the other.

On our walk back to the gatehouse, we turned left at the intersection so we could find another entrance to the Castle Garth. Other people were out in the Garth today with some walking their dogs. It wasn't long until we were at the entrance to the gatehouse yard.

"What are we going to do now?" Katie asked.

I looked at my phone for the time. I needed to study up on Wolsey and get my head clear for the visit. I looked at Sara. "Why don't you girls go to outlet mall again by Uber while I stay here and plan an outing for tomorrow?" I had remembered the 42 Bus didn't run on Sunday.

"Yes!" Ashlynn and Katie shouted almost in unison. Sara didn't look as enthusiastic.

"I'll go," Sara said, "but you girls can't go wild in wanting stuff. Your budget is limited."

"And remember, whatever you buy has to be small enough to fit in your suitcase when we leave for home," I added.

We all waited on the sidewalk outside the gatehouse yard where the 42 bus stop was for the Uber. When it came and the girls got in, I waved a goodbye and turned back toward the gatehouse.

I walked to the roof first to see if it was ready for Wolsey's visit. I stepped from side to side to get a view of the village and the route that Wolsey had taken when he was arrested and on his way to London to be tried for treason. I took a piece of paper and pen in my hand to write a few questions I might ask Wolsey.

When I got back down to our room, I noticed a leaflet that John Cattanach had given me about walking around the village. I looked it over and took a walk. Sometimes I could think and clear my mind better when I strolled through the grass or along the sidewalks. It would be a refreshing time for me while the girls were away shopping.

My adventure took me down the street toward the Ferry Inn and along that street toward a cemetery on my left. I walked through it for a bit to see if I recognized any names on the gravestones. I looked again at the map of the walk and noticed that there was a Wolsey Avenue not far up the street from the Jolly Sailor. I turned and walked in that direction. At least the village had not forgotten Wolsey.

I walked for two hours before returning to the gatehouse for a nap. My sheet of paper was full of questions and observations for Wolsey.

Sara and the girls returned with their purchases and enough food for us to have for dinner.

"Look at this dress," Katie said and held up a pretty pink dress in front of her.

"And I bought a helmet for horse riding," Ashlynn said. She held up the shiny blue helmet that said "York" in bright silver letters on both sides. After showing me their purchases, both girls headed up to their room.

Sara now had become accustomed to my early morning visits with spirits and did not try to dissuade me from my meeting with Wolsey. After another blaze in the fireplace and glasses of wine, we retired to bed around 10 p.m.

I tried going to sleep while wondering whether Servant really would bring Wolsey to the roof. I turned from side to side before falling asleep. I awoke at 2 a.m. and looked at my phone. Too early, I thought. But I eased out of bed and went and sat in front of the fireplace where wood embers still sparkled. A half hour later and a half hour early for our meeting, I made my way to the roof.

The night air was crisp. The five chairs still sat where I left them. There was no rain or cloudiness. The stars and moon provided a ghostly light to the top of the roof. I walked from side to side, looking over the parapet on each side. Lights from the village houses marked the location of streets. One car came up to Thorpe Lane and turned toward the bridge over the River Ouse. I took my paper with my notes and went and sat in the far chair in the row of three. I would wait.

True to his punctuality, Servant appeared shortly on the other end leaving the middle chair for our hoped-for guest.

"Servant, how are you?" I thought, and he heard. "I saw you at All Saints Church earlier."

"What a nice service," I heard him say. "John and George also enjoyed it."

"Will Wolsey come?" I asked.

"He's on his way from Leicester," Servant answered. "And guess who else I found for a later visit?"

"Who"

"Catherine Howard and Thomas Culpeper."

"Really?"

"Yes. Remember, they came here with King Henry the Eighth. Unfortunately, Henry believed them to be having an affair and had them both executed shortly after their visit."

"What about King Henry? Any luck with getting him here?"

"No. He said he would only leave Hampton Court Palace and come here by an Order of the Great Spirit."

"And what is the chance of getting that?" I asked.

"I'm praying on it," Servant said. "I'm sure Wolsey, Catherine, and Thomas would like to see him and get their hands on him—if they had hands."

"Maybe we can get the Great Spirit to order them all to come at the same time."

"That's an idea," Servant said. "Perhaps they could voice their grievances with Henry."

"Sort of like put him on trial," I added.

Just then the middle chair filled with the spirit of Cardinal Thomas Wolsey. His robe appeared to be more silver—polished silver that reflected the stars. He rose from his chair and moved across the roof to each of the four sides, as I had done when I first came up. After pausing at each side for a minute, he returned to the middle chair. It seemed he turned toward Servant and then me.

"That was where I rode out of the castle on my mule when the king had me arrested," I heard him say in a very soft voice. "Thank you for inviting me back. Leicester Abbey is no more, and my grave is not properly marked. How low the high has fallen."

I could tell he was in one sense happy about coming back to Cawood Castle, but he was also forlorn about what had happened to him.

"I understand you worked diligently on repairing and restoring Cawood Castle when you lived here in 1529 and 1530 until your arrest in November of that year." I tried to be as kind as I could.

"It was in a pitiful shape of disrepair and deterioration when I arrived. I was familiar with more grand surroundings. I had Hampton Palace built for me. And I also had other buildings refurbished and updated.

"I immediately began to make Cawood Castle a magnificent abode when I arrived in 1529. But it was not to be. The project would take years. I left in 1530 under the escort of the king's men. The people of the village loved me. They saw what I was building. I employed many of them in the repairs."

"I know you were appointed Archbishop of York in 1514 and became a Cardinal in 1515. But you didn't come here immediately upon your appointment."

"No. I only came to Yorkshire in 1529. I was busy with the King's work."

"As several of the Archbishops of York, you were appointed as Lord Chancellor in 1515 by the king."

"Yes. For many years, I was second in command. There was King Henry. Then there was me. I was in well with Pope Leo the Tenth who made me a Cardinal. At Henry's request, I prosecuted many of those he opposed. I helped with the English campaign in France and the peace negotiations after. Pope Leo also appointed me as Papal Legate, which meant I made many religious decisions."

"You helped to arrange the Field of the Cloth of Gold in 1520."

"That was a rather flamboyant affair. We showed off the wealth of England by trying to influence other European nations. We had over five thousand followers there."

"You aligned with Spain."

"Probably a mistake. France may have been a better ally."

"You worked with King Henry the Eighth for many years. What do you think of him?" I looked directly at Wolsey. He seemed to shift in his chair and shuffle around a bit. I may have brought up a touchy subject.

"He was a murderer, a thief, an adulterer, and a father of bastard children. Besides that, he was a pretty nice man."

I looked over at Servant. Should I continue down this road? Servant looked away, giving me no answer. So, I pressed on.

"Tell me about what brought King Henry to take away your privileges and charge you with treason."

"Henry could always change the definition of treason to fit his purposes. Of course, he was angry with me because I could not secure an annulment between him and Katherine of Aragon, his first wife."

“It was a long and drawn-out matter. Katherine’s father had influence with the Pope as much as I did. She did not want or agree to an annulment. We tried over a period of years to get one. I even argued what Henry wanted me to about Leviticus, even though I knew it did not apply.”

“How was that?” I asked.

“Henry’s older brother, Arthur, was only fourteen when he and Katherine were married. He died at fifteen years of age. Katherine said they never consummated the marriage.

“Henry relied on Leviticus 20:21, which I can just about quote from memory: ‘If a man takes his brother’s wife, it is an unclean thing. He has uncovered his brother’s nakedness. They shall die childless.’

“That was what Henry wanted to use to get the annulment so he could marry Anne Boleyn. Henry and Katherine didn’t have any male children. Henry desperately wanted a male child to succeed him.

“The problem with using the Leviticus verse was that it said ‘wife’ and not ‘widow.’ It was speaking about having relations with the brother’s wife while they were both living. I could not get this through Henry’s head. He thought that was why he didn’t have a male heir by Katherine. They had the daughter, Mary, but Henry didn’t think the people would accept a woman to be their leader. Mary became queen and tried to restore Catholicism as the national religion—killing many protestants in her wake and being called Bloody Mary.

“Also, he only used one verse to prove his point. If he had read further, he would have found verses that not only allowed brothers to marry a deceased brother's wife or widow, but encouraged it if the brother died without children, as Arthur did.

"Deuteronomy 25:5 says: 'If brothers dwell together, and one of them dies and has no child, the wife of the dead shall not marry without unto a stranger: her husband's brother shall go in unto her, and take her to him to wife, and perform the duty of a husband's brother unto her.'

"But Henry, like so many others, took one verse and read no further."

"So, Henry banished you from his presence. But why did he charge you with treason?"

"Henry could change the definition of treason on a whim and almost instantaneously. He said I was corresponding with the French to plot his overthrow.

"Remember, Henry had many people executed including those of his closest advisors, including some during my time and some afterward—Thomas More, Thomas Cromwell, and Thomas Cranmer, among others.

"Anne Boleyn joined in plotting against me since I couldn't procure the annulment that would allow her to marry Henry. Of course, they did later on. That didn't turn out very well for Anne. She lost her head on the block. Also, later, after I was gone, Catherine Howard and Thomas Culpeper lost their heads."

I looked over again at Servant. Should I tell Cardinal Wolsey that Catherine Howard and Thomas Culpeper had visited the Cawood Castle with King Henry and were going to come back for another visit? I went ahead and told him.

"That's good," he said. "They can tell you a lot more about Henry's murderous ways. Maybe we all can get together and bring Henry back so we could talk with him."

"Or put him on trial for all his misdeeds," I said. When I looked at Servant, he seemed to nod his head. "What were you talking about when you said that Henry was not only a murderer, but also a thief?" I asked Cardinal Wolsey.

"And quite a thief at that. I was a fairly wealthy man myself after years of serving Henry and being a Cardinal and Archbishop. I liked to build things. I possessed Hampton Court Palace when it was but a small manor house in 1514. I constructed a magnificent palace around it beginning the next year. We had grand parties there for royalty and foreign kings and queens. I even arranged for it to have running water flowing through from the river.

"When Henry saw it while at the parties, he decided he wanted it to be his. He asked me to give it to him. What could I do? If the king asks you for something, you're pretty much obliged to give it or lose your head. So, he got it. I call it a theft since I built it, and he didn't pay me what it was worth."

"Any other thefts?" I asked.

"Well, after I died, and he took over the church. That was a theft from Rome. Then he closed the monasteries and robbed them of all their precious possessions. He said he was doing it for the country, but he kept a lot for himself. The monasteries controlled a great deal of land. Henry profited greatly from that theft. He said he did it as Supreme Head of the Church."

"We've been trying to get King Henry to come back here for a visit, but so far, he has refused. He had been at the Cawood Castle with Catherine Howard and Thomas Culpeper on the Progress to the North and a hunting trip in 1541," I said.

"That was after my time," Cardinal Wolsey responded. "But if you ever get him here, I would like to come back to confront him. And if you could get a trial for him, I would like to be the prosecutor.

I prosecuted a lot of his enemies for him. Now, I would like to prosecute him."

I nodded my head and looked at my notes. "You said he was an adulterer. Is that true? Ha, Ha," I laughed at my own question as I knew King Henry's history.

"Henry had Ann Boleyn and Catherine Howard executed for adultery. He said adultery against him was treason. But when he did it, he considered it his right.

"Henry thought the Ladies in Waiting for his queens were his private harem—they were 'in waiting' for him. I don't know how many he had affairs with and had children by. He recognized at least one child and named him Henry Fitzroy," Cardinal Wolsey said and looked both at me and Servant.

I sat there quietly for a minute, letting Wolsey settle down a bit. Then I moved on. "Were you surprised when they came to arrest you?"

"Certainly. I knew I had been banished to the north to Yorkshire, but I never thought Henry would charge me with treason after all I had done for him. Servant was here when they came for me. All the village was in an uproar when they found out. They loved me. Your young ancestor, John Cawood, who later became a printer for royalty in London was here. He was only fifteen years old, but he was a very bright young man and visited the castle very often.

"When Henry Percy, Earl of Northumberland, and Walter Walsh rode in with others of the king's men, I first thought they were coming for a social visit. I invited them to dine with me. Then Percy made it known to me that he had come to arrest me for treason.

"I was greatly distressed, to say the least. I knew what Henry did to those charged with treason. There would be no actual trial. I would enjoy a brief stay at the Tower of London before they lopped off my head. The arrest announcement ruined our dinner.

"The next morning, we all set out for London. We rode right through this gatehouse. Me on my mule and all the king's men on their beautiful horses. It seemed that they regretted their task, but there was nothing they could do. As the verse goes, 'all the King's men and all the King's horses couldn't put me back together again' the way I had been in years past with King Henry.

"It was November and desperately cold. I was able to bring with me Edmund Bonner, my personal chaplain. A large crowd from the village greeted me as I passed through the gatehouse. But then it was a dreary ride toward London.

"By the time we reached Leicester, I was dreadfully sick. Thinking about my fate did not raise my spirits. We stayed at Leicester Abbey. I told those who were looking after me at the abbey: 'I see the matter against me, how it is framed. But if I had served God as diligently as I have done the King, he would not have given me over in my grey hairs.'

"I died there. Better to die peacefully there than to go to the Tower. I was only fifty-seven."

It was a sad tale. I shuffled in my chair. It was probably time to let Cardinal Wolsey go back to Leicester or wherever he wanted.

"Thanks for coming. Your story is compelling. We will definitely invite you back if we can get King Henry here for a visit or trial, as it may be."

It was only a minute before the spirit of Cardinal Wolsey left the chair and ascended until the gentle wind took him toward Leicester. His bright silver likeness shown like a star.

I looked over at Servant. "That was a great visit. Thank you."

Servant looked away and then back at me. "I was seventy-seven when they came and arrested the Cardinal. I walked on a cane. It was probably my saddest time at the Castle."

I waited a bit. Then I asked. "When will Catherine Howard and Thomas Culpeper visit?"

"It will have to be two nights from now. A little more planning is involved."

"What about Henry?"

"I will petition the Great Spirit to order him here—for a visit and trial."

Chapter Nine

Catherine Howard and Thomas Culpeper

Servant gave me two days to think about the visit of Catherine Howard and Thomas Culpeper. We had been meeting almost daily. What was I going to do with the extra time? Getting nervous and worried for two things—and maybe they combined into one.

I was not as much nervous and worried about the visit of the two young lovers—Howard and Culpeper—as I was about the prospect that King Henry VIII might visit. All the other ghosts or spirits had been nice and friendly. But I knew of King Henry's reputation for wrath when someone crossed him. But as a spirit, was he the same?

Servant had said earlier that the Great Spirit had sent King Henry to America for a hundred years leading up to the Revolution to be among people who did not want a king and who revolted against England. But now Henry had been hanging out at his former palace of Hampton Court Palace.

A hot pot of coffee perked, and two pieces of toast popped up. Maybe these would distract me from my concerns. Sara joined me at the table.

"How did it go with Cardinal Wolsey?" she asked.

I could tell by the tone of her voice that she was still skeptical that I was meeting with spirits or the ghosts of Cawood Castle.

"It was my best meeting so far. He was very forthcoming about his downfall, his time at the castle, and his relationship with Henry the Eighth."

"Oh, did he like King Henry?"

"At first, he was a loyal right-hand man to the king. But, of course, their relationship soured toward the end."

"And he was arrested for treason right here at the castle?"

"Yes. But he died at Leicester Abbey before getting to London. He knew what awaited him."

Sara put her cup of coffee down and looked me in the eye. "Do you really believe you are meeting with these spirits?"

"Yes."

"Have you ever thought that maybe you have studied and researched them so much that they appear to be real but are only figments of your imagination? That you are so obsessed with them that they appear in your mind but are not real?"

"I believe they are real. I have seen and heard them."

"But nobody else has. You saw them at the church, but I didn't."

"I guess I have received a special dispensation."

"And you're going to a psychiatrist when we get home."

"And guess who is coming in a couple of days."

"Who?"

"Queen Catherine Howard and Thomas Culpeper."

"Oh, in a couple of days? You don't have a meeting with anyone in the morning?"

"No. Servant needed some time to make the arrangements. But then we're hoping to have King Henry come for a visit after that."

"Hoping? Servant doesn't have it arranged?"

"No. King Henry is obstinate. He won't come without an order."

"An order? From whom?" Sara asked.

"From the Great Spirit."

"God?"

"Yes. If we get King Henry here, Servant and I are planning for some others—like Wolsey, Catherine Howard and Thomas Culpeper—to come back for a little sit-down conversation with the King. Or a trial."

"A trial? For all his crimes? Who would be the judge and jury?"

"We'll have to work on that. Wolsey agreed to be the prosecutor."

We looked toward the stairway as we heard the granddaughters walking from their room.

"We'll have to talk more about your visions later," Sara said.

"Where are we going today?" Katie asked.

"Well, we have a couple of days to do what you girls want. What do you suggest?" I asked.

"I want to go back to York and walk those walls that I saw," Katie answered.

"I'd like that, too," Ashlynn said. "And I'd like to find a place to ride horses so I can wear my new helmet."

"We'll have to work on the horse riding. I know they have a lot of races in York. There may be a place there we can find. Get ready and we'll catch the 42 bus to York," I said.

The girls got ready in record time. The 42 bus arrived outside the castle fence within fifteen minutes. After we turned across the bridge over the River Ouse, Ashlynn kept her eyes trained for horses. She was serious about wanting to ride.

We alighted again at the Piccadilly stop in York. The girls were old enough to go on their own to walk the ancient walls of York while Sara and I walked a slower route through the Shambles area—shops fronting the street where butchering facilities had been in ancient times.

"See that McDonald's?" I asked before the girls sprinted away. "We'll meet there in three hours. Don't be late, and don't get lost."

They began walking toward the walls while Sara and I checked our street map for what was on the Shambles. Many shops were there now—but no butchers as in the days of old. The map had a note that the street was very narrow so that little sunlight would get to the displayed meat of the butcher shops.

Now, the shops were a tourist attraction. There were jewelry shops, cafes, and a Viking goods store, among others. We walked into the Parlormade Café and had a cup of tea and a scone each. Sara looked into the shop of British wool and cashmere. The York Viking shop was interesting, but I wasn't sure how I could get metal objects through airport security. The short street looked to be not much longer than an American football field and end zones. However, it was packed with shops and people.

"I would like to go back to the York Minster," I told Sara.

"Why? We've already been there."

I pulled a sheet of paper from my pocket. "I want to see if I can find the burial places of the archbishops who came to visit me on the roof."

"You think they would be there to talk with you?" Sara asked.

"I had thought about that, but I don't know."

"There're some shops here and up the street that I can go to while you do that. I'll meet you and the girls at McDonald's."

I paid my entrance and tour fee at York Minster, and then I took off to explore on my own.

Looking at my notes, I walked toward the eastern part of the North Transept to look for William Greenfield's crypt. I thought I found it and continued my walk around the North Aisle of the Nave to William Melton's grave site.

William Zouche was buried before the Altar of Saint Edward in the Nave. John Thoresby's place was before the Altar of the Virgin in the Lady Chapel. Thomas Rotherham had a magnificent marble tomb. I wondered if that was because he died of the plague and wasn't buried here until five years after his death.

Having walked almost the full circuit of the Minster, I sat down and waited. And waited. And waited. I looked at my phone. I only had fifteen minutes before I was to meet Sara and the girls. No spirits appeared. Perhaps they were all out visiting other places. When none of the archbishops' spirits appeared, or even Servant's spirit, I decided it was time to leave. I was rather disappointed in not seeing the spirits, but I also was delighted that I found most of their resting places.

Sara and the girls were already at McDonald's when I arrived.

"We liked the walk on the walls," Katie said.

"And, Bobo, we found out where a horse-riding stable is," Ashlynn added.

"And I found a jewelry shop," Sara said and showed me her new silver bracelet.

"I'm glad everyone had a good time," I said. "And where is the horse place?"

"They said it's near the racetrack. Within a mile," Ashlynn said. "Can we go now?"

I looked at the time. "Not today. But I will take you tomorrow. You can bring your new helmet."

"You promise?" Ashlynn asked.

"Yes."

We finished our lunch and walked to the nearest stop for the 42 bus. Back at the castle gatehouse, the girls went to their room while Sara and I sat in front of the fireplace.

"You don't have any meetings with spirits in the early morning?" Sara asked.

"No. One more day until Catherine and Thomas come. I believe I'll start another fire in the fireplace. We can take the girls horse riding tomorrow, and I'll prepare for my meeting."

The girls were up early the next morning. Ashlynn was wearing her new helmet. Katie said she would have to borrow one at the stables.

This was probably the most relaxing and fun day for the girls. They rode the horses for over three hours. Sara and I strolled over to the racetrack where they were preparing for a big race day the next day. York, it turned out, was one of the largest horse racetracks in England. People came from all over to watch the horses, drink a few pints, and bet a little. It was like the Kentucky Derby without the big hats.

By dark, we had eaten dinner and were back to the gatehouse. It was early to bed for all of us as my thoughts turned toward the arrival of my guests on the roof of the gatehouse.

"Be careful up there," Sara said before she went to sleep. "Remember, those two lost their heads because of what they did here at the castle."

Near the appointed time, I rolled out of bed and went to the stairway. This was getting to be a regular ritual. I stepped softly on the stone stairway that was spiraling me toward the door to the roof. Out into the darkness, I went to the chairs and rearranged them a bit. I put two facing another two just a few feet apart. Servant and I would sit next to each other facing the other two chairs that I had designated for Catherine Howard and Thomas Culpeper. Then I walked softly to my chair and took a seat.

Servant appeared on time and sat next to me. "Good morning," I heard him say.

"And they are coming?" I asked in my thoughts.

"Yes. They will be here shortly."

"I had a relaxing two days. We went to York. I found most of the resting places for the archbishops at York Minster. Then the next day, the girls got to go horse riding."

"Delightful," Servant said.

Then I thought I heard a rush of wind. The two chairs facing us were filled with bright colored robes—one was pink and the other one was blue. I decided those colors would indicate the male and female of our guests.

Servant spoke first. "So happy that you could come, Lady Catherine and Lord Culpeper."

It appeared that the heads of the robes nodded in acknowledgment. But it also seemed that the heads of the robes were a bit separated from the bodies of the robes. Perhaps that was because our guests' heads had been severed from their physical bodies at their deaths.

Catherine, in the pink robe, looked at me. "Thanks for inviting us back to where we had a few happy moments."

I wasn't sure how to approach the ones who I thought were lovers at Cawood Castle in 1541. But I jumped in.

"Tell us about how you came to be here at Cawood Castle in 1541."

"Henry and I married in July 1540. I was seventeen and he was forty-nine. We married less than three weeks after his annulment of his marriage to Anne of Cleaves. That was 28 July 1540—the same day he had Thomas Cromwell executed. Henry never hesitated mixing death with marriage.

"The next year, he wanted to go on a what they called the Royal Progress to the North. He hoped to meet King James the

Fifth of Scotland. It was good to get out of London with all the death and bad smells. We set off on 30 June 1541. There was a great entourage that went with us—including my favorite, Thomas Culpeper."

With that said, she turned toward the blue-robed Culpeper.

"So, you visited other areas of Yorkshire besides coming here to the Cawood Castle?"

"Yes. It was quite a trip. And every place we lodged was a beautiful castle or palace—and Thomas was always there. There were nearly four thousand people with us. The supply wagons came behind us, lining the roads for a mile or two. At every palace and castle where we stopped, many had to sleep and lodge in the courtyards and fields. The butchers, bakers, and cooks had quite a job.

"The entire trip went on from June through September."

"Did you enjoy your visit here to Cawood Castle?" I asked.

"Enjoy it!? We had a party every evening. Henry would go out hunting with many of the men. Thomas and I would stay here and enjoy ourselves."

"You had been married for almost a year. Were you pregnant by Henry?"

"Oh, no."

"Did you have a coronation?"

"No. That was to wait until I was pregnant, but I never was. All I got was a barge ride down the Thames to the Traitors' Gate at the Tower when I was charged with treason."

I moved on to perhaps a more pleasant subject. "Describe Henry for me," I requested.

"Oh, my. How can I say this? By 1541, Henry was disgustingly fat. He had a belly like a keg of ale. Two of his attendants had to help him mount his horse to go riding and hunting. He had open sores on his leg from his long-ago accident while jousting. They smelled worse than the black death. He weighed twenty-three stones."

I glanced at my phone to find out how many pounds a 'stone' was. The answer I got was fourteen pounds per 'stone.' I quickly multiplied fourteen by twenty-three to see how much she was alleging Henry weighed at that time. The answer was three hundred and twenty-two pounds.

"So, he wasn't particularly attractive at that time?"

"He wore fine clothes, hats, and such. He still wanted hosiery that displayed his large calves. But to a seventeen-year-old young lady, he was not physically attractive. Why didn't he find a queen of his own age? I'll answer that myself. He wanted someone young enough to bear him a son. That wasn't going to be me."

"So, you looked to younger companions?" I asked.

"Thomas was my primary companion. We had to sneak around. Henry always had someone watching. But we found time together, didn't we, Thomas?"

Culpeper had remained silent while Catherine had talked. Now, he turned toward her and then toward us.

"If Catherine had not written letters to me expressing her love, I don't think we would have been found out. I always said our meetings were to do with matters concerning England. Of course, those were lies."

Then Catherine broke in.

"Thomas was twenty-six. He had a ruddy complexion, slender, and a head full of hair. His precious blue eyes captivated me."

I could tell that they had a deep affection for each other—love—that led to both of them losing their heads a short time after visiting Cawood Castle. I looked at Culpeper.

"What did you think of King Henry?"

He hesitated for a minute and appeared to turn around as though looking for King Henry or a spy.

"I was an up and comer in the King's view at first. I was a member of the King's Gentlemen of the Privy Chamber and advised the king on many things. I was a collector of rare items, and I gave many to him to gain his favor. I was one of the many that he took on his Royal Progress to the North. I tried to get lost in the crowd when I wanted to see Catherine.

"But I knew that King Henry was a wrathful man. He had Thomas Cromwell executed on the same day he married Catherine. Cromwell was his closest advisor for a while after Cardinal Wolsey. So, I should have known my head was in danger if I ever crossed him. But I continued my intrigue with the King's wife.

"What did I think of him? He was deceitful, greedy, obnoxious, ostentatious, murderous, adulterer, hateful, disgusting, loathsome, and nasty."

I gathered that Culpeper did not care much for Henry in the end. I looked next to me at Servant who had not moved or spoken during my interviews. He nodded for me to go ahead.

I looked at Catherine. She had already mentioned her arrest for treason and being taken to the Tower of London for execution.

"Lady Howard, I want to ask you about a quote that has been attributed to you at the time of your execution. Someone has written that on the execution platform, one of your last utterances was this: 'I die a queen, but I would rather die the wife of Thomas Culpeper.'"

"Ha, ha. That sounds like something I should have said, but I don't remember saying it. I was very nervous and scared about losing my head."

Servant looked toward me. I heard him whisper to conclude our interview and ask our visitors about coming back.

"Would you two be willing to return here if we could get King Henry here? We were thinking about asking him a few things about his conduct—with you, Wolsey, and others. So far, he has declined our invitations to visit. But Servant has requested the Great Spirit to order Henry back to get an explanation of his conduct. Like a trial. Wolsey has agreed to be the prosecutor. You two could be witnesses."

The pink and blue robes turned toward each other. Then it was like their hands joined.

"We'd be delighted!" they said in unison.

"Servant will tell you when. Thank you for coming, and I look forward to seeing you in the near future."

With that said, they went up and over the roof wall. I turned to Servant.

"We have a lot of planning to do for the trial of Henry the Eighth."

"Let's meet again here tomorrow morning and do our planning," Servant said.

Chapter Ten

Pre-Trial

"So, how did your meeting go with the young lovers?" Sara asked when we sat with our coffee at mid-morning.

"Their story could have been a Shakesperean Tragedy," I said. "She was barely eighteen when she died. Culpeper was just twenty-seven. Both fell from high positions. She was queen. He was high up in the royal court. They got together. Henry charged them with treason because of their affair. No real trial. Both were beheaded. Culpeper's head was put on a spike on Tower Bridge."

"They were executed for adultery?" Sara asked.

"Adultery was the same as treason in Henry's eyes," I answered.

"That's terrible."

"But guess what."

"What?" Sara asked.

"They are both coming back when we have a trial on the roof for King Henry!"

"A trial? I thought Henry wouldn't come. What changed his mind?"

"Servant is talking to the Great Spirit to get Henry here. Wolsey has agreed to be the prosecutor. Howard and Culpeper are coming back as witnesses."

"You're getting crazier and crazier," Sara said. "God is going to send King Henry the Eighth back here?"

"Just his spirit."

"How do you try a spirit?" Sara asked

"With other spirits—and me, I guess."

"And what will be your role? Remember, Henry is not one to be taken lightly. Even his spirit may find a way to do away with you."

"I'm not sure what my role will be. I am a lawyer. So, maybe I could keep the trial moving along legally. Servant and I are going to work out the details in the morning."

Sara shook her head and stared out the window. "I'll be happy when we go home, and I can get you to a psychiatrist. These episodes you're having with ghosts or spirits is troublesome, to say the least."

Then the girls came down from their room.

"What are we doing today?" Katie asked while Ashlynn stood behind her.

"We have a free day. What would you like to do?" I asked.

"Let's go back to the outlet mall," Katie said, and Ashlynn nodded her head.

"Sounds like a good idea," I said. "I'll go too this time."

Going shopping at the mall was always a good idea for the girls. I could take the day off, stroll through the mall, and think about the trial to come.

"Get ready, and we'll catch the 42," I said. The girls ran back upstairs to get ready for the trip while Sara and I dressed in our room.

When we were on the 42 and turned onto the bridge over the River Ouse, I tried to imagine how King Henry the Eighth, Catherine Howard, Thomas Culpeper, and their entourage of nearly four thousand crossed the river in 1541. Or did they? Most sources say they turned toward Hull and later crossed the Derwent where there was a bridge. It would have taken a full day just to get to the other side of the River Ouse since there was no bridge here at that time.

They also must have followed close to the route that we were taking. I had read that they had proceeded up the road to Fulford before arriving at York. The roads were paved now. Then they were probably dirt with some gravel. It was quite a procession.

I was actually looking forward to going to the outlet mall. My mind and my efforts had been concentrated on genealogy, family, history, buildings, ghosts, and spirits for the whole trip. At the mall, I could do what ordinary people do. I had also missed the exposure of my physical senses to experiencing things and forces other than sight and sound. My meetings with the spirits had engaged my sight and sound, through mental telepathy. But I had missed the aromas of bread baking and touching textured cloth.

We walked to the entrance from the bus stop and entered a different world from the castle gatehouse or the York Minster. I could see why the girls wanted to come back even if they purchased little. This was the modern world and not ancient history. They were right at home in walking to and past all the shops.

"Two hours," I told Katie and Ashlynn. "You stay together. You can look and pick out an item or two. Then when we meet back here, we'll all go and purchase those items if they're not too expensive. Your Nana and I will take our time walking the hallways and looking."

With that said, they were off on a fast walk down the hallway.

"I smell a food court," I told Sara. The aromas of freshly cooked donuts and of peppers and onions frying led me down the walkway. I thought I smelled chicken frying. This was something I could enjoy.

"You want food already?" Sara asked.

"No. Those aromas are just leading me that way."

"Let's walk by a few shops before we sit down to eat anything," she said.

It appeared that there were at least ten stores between us and where the hallway angled off toward the food court. We entered each one. I ran my fingers across ridged fabric of vests and trousers. I picked up a vase in one shop that had an engraving of York Minster. At another shop, the clerks were spraying samples of perfume and cologne on anyone who obliged and held out their wrists. The aroma I received certainly improved my sweaty hand. At another boutique they had a display of scented candles.

"We need to get a couple of these to take back to the gatehouse," I told Sara. "When we don't have a fire in the fireplace, we can have light and fragrance from the candles."

"You romantic soul," Sara said and nodded her head. "We'll get two or three before we leave."

Having spent the better part of an hour exploring the outlet shops, we turned into the food court. I ordered unhealthy food—fried donuts and coffee. Sara had a nice chicken salad.

When we met the girls after the allotted two hours, they herded us back to a jewelry store where each had us purchase a small silver bracelet for them that had the word "York" in sparkly letters. We stopped at the candle shop and bought four wide candles that had an apple aroma to take back to the gatehouse.

The girls were satisfied with their purchases. Sara and I arranged the four candles beneath the two large windows in our room. We retired for the night. My meeting on the roof with Servant would happen again in the early morning hours.

Before getting into bed, I lit the candles—two on each side.

"Do you think it will be safe to leave them burning all night?" Sara asked.

"I think so. And I will check them when I get up to meet Servant."

At a few minutes before our meeting time. I was up. The candles gave off an orange flickering glow. I went to each and extinguished their flame. The aroma of apples rose in the spiraling whisps of smoke. I took a piece of paper and a pen with me as I ascended the stairs. I opened the door to the roof quietly so as not to awaken the girls.

The five chairs were still arranged in the middle of the roof. It was silent except for the sound of a car toward Selby. I had learned that crickets and frogs generally retired before this hour. The moon wasn't full, but it was nearly so. Stars shone through gently rolling clouds. I sat down and waited. What would this place be like if we had a trial for King Henry? Was there room here?

At that moment, Servant arrived in the chair next to me.

"How did your day go?" he asked.

"Fine. A trip to the outlet mall. Time with the family," I answered in my head. "Are we on for King Henry?"

"Yes. The Great Spirit ordered him to appear here two mornings away."

I slapped my knees in excitement. "What time?"

"Earlier. Just after midnight. It will give us more hours of darkness to get Henry's story or to try him."

I thought: What would we need to have here to try him?

Servant received the thought and answered. "We will need a jury. We will need witnesses. We will need Wolsey as the prosecutor. We will need a judge."

"The only witnesses we have are Catherine and Thomas," I said.

"Wolsey can be a witness also," Servant said.

"Can he be a witness and the prosecutor?" I asked.

"Why not? You are the judge," Servant answered.

"Me--as judge? How can that work? Everyone else is a spirit. I'm a physical human."

"You are a lawyer. You're experienced in court procedure. You can just keep the trial moving along with the jury to make the final decision."

"Will Henry go for that?"

"He has no choice. The Great Spirit has told him to come," Servant said.

"A jury?" I asked. "Where are we going to get a jury of twelve?"

"Think back to our visits with other spirits," Servant said. "Who have joined us on the roof or in front of the fireplace?"

I started counting in my mind. George Neville, the three kings, the seven archbishops, and John Kemp. I had talked with twelve spirits here at the castle gatehouse. That was the exact number we needed for a modern jury.

"Yes, you have counted correctly," Servant said.

"And what will be your role?" I asked Servant.

"You might say that I will be the bailiff. I will be responsible for getting all the spirits here as I have done in the past. I will call the court to order. I will swear in the witnesses. Whatever else is needed," Servant said.

I looked around the rooftop. We only had five chairs. Again, I started counting in my head. We needed twelve chairs for the jury. Culpeper and Howard should each have a chair—as would Wolsey. Henry would want a fine chair. We needed another chair for me if I was going to be the judge. And finally, Servant would need a chair.

"Eighteen chairs!" I shouted. "We only have five here. Thirteen more chairs are what we need."

"You're very good at math," Servant said. I noticed a smile on his countenance. "You can have them delivered from a party shop in

Selby. Ring them up in a few hours and they will be here before nightfall."

This sounded like a big production to me. Chairs and seventeen spirits on the roof along with me. I nodded my head and made notes on my sheet of paper. At least I had two days to get it arranged.

"Anything else?" I asked Servant.

"A gavel—and you need one of those white judge's wigs like they have used in English Courts for a few hundred years."

My hands went to my head. I couldn't imagine me wearing the white wig of a judge. I looked over toward Servant, but he was gone.

Chapter Eleven

The Trial of King Henry VIII

I continued to sit on the darkened rooftop after Servant had left. What was I to do? A trial of Henry the Eighth in two days. I was to be the judge. There was to be a jury of nine archbishops and three kings.

Servant said for me to get a judge's gavel and a white wig like the ones worn by English judges. I took my phone and clicked on Google. Fortunately, I had a good signal on the rooftop. My search for "English Judges' Wigs" brought up several. I clicked on the one on Amazon and ordered it for overnight delivery. I looked a bit further and found the gavel I needed. Why not go all the way, I thought? I found a black judge's robe.

Before I left the site, I had to pay and say where to deliver the items. I thought for a minute. The castle gatehouse might not be the best and most expeditious. Then it struck me. The Pickled Postie was a post office and had a well-known address. After a few more clicks, including my credit card payment, it was done. Delivery was guaranteed within twenty-four hours. I would walk to the Pickled Postie when they opened and tell them to expect my delivery.

I again looked online for the party store in Selby that Servant had mentioned. I found one that had tents, tables, and chairs for parties. I would ring them up later in the morning. I decided on eleven more folding chairs. Then the one for King Henry would be a bit more elegant and sturdier. If he weighed three hundred twenty pounds at his death, how large would his spirit be? A wide chair was needed. And for me as judge, I should be seated in a chair that showed authority. I found one that had blue upholstery. That would be it. But I needed to be seated a bit above the jury and witnesses. I needed some type of platform. What I found were two wooden pallets that were used to hold things in transport. They would do. No need to go overboard.

Back downstairs and to bed for a few hours. My mind rolled with the things I had to do and the order to make at the party store. Delivery to the castle gatehouse roof might be a little problem. I would have to tell Sara what I was expecting. I would suggest that she and the girls go out for the day until I arranged everything on the roof.

When the sun was fully up, I went to make our morning coffee. Sara was up soon, and we sat at the table, each of us sipping our cups of coffee.

"What did you and Servant get planned?" Sara asked.

"We're all set. King Henry will be sent here. We're having a trial."

"On the roof?"

"Yes. Twelve jurors, Servant as bailiff, Wolsey as prosecutor, Howard and Culpeper as witnesses, and me as judge."

"Who chose you to be judge?" Sara asked.

"It just sort of fell to me. I didn't particularly want to do it, but that's the way it worked out."

"A human judging a spirit? How does that work?"

"The jury will make any decisions. I will just make sure the proceedings move along—legally."

Sara shook her head and looked down at her cup of coffee.

"I ordered a white judge's wig, a gavel, and a black judicial robe," I said.

"What?"

"They are to be delivered to the Pickled Postie today or tomorrow in time for the trial which is two mornings away."

"I can't believe it," Sara said.

"And I'm ordering some chairs from a party store in Selby for the jury, witnesses, prosecutor and me. I need you to take the girls on a day-long excursion so that they can be delivered to the roof without the girls knowing that I'm meeting with ghosts."

While Sara mulled that over in her head, I took my phone and called the party store. They would deliver the chairs near 3 p.m. and they would give me two wooden pallets at no charge.

The girls sprinted into our room. "What's on for today?" Ashlynn asked.

"You girls want to walk with me to the Pickled Postie for breakfast?" I asked. I needed to make the clerk aware of my delivery from Amazon, and going for breakfast would give me a chance.

"What about after that?" Katie asked.

I thought of York and the River Ouse. There were boat rides there.

"Would you like to go to York with Nana and take a boat ride for a few hours? And maybe stop by the outlet mall on your way back?"

"That sounds like fun," Katie said.

I looked at Sara. She nodded her reluctant agreement.

A few minutes later at the Pickled Postie, I told the young lady behind the counter that I was expecting a delivery from Amazon later in the day or early the next day. I gave her my number to text when it arrived. Then the girls and I sat down for breakfast.

By noon Sara and the girls had taken off on the 42 toward York. I would await the delivery of the chairs and arrange them on the roof. Then I remembered that I had ordered a gavel, but what would I use to bang it on if needed? I looked around our room. Near one window was a pedestal holding a vase on top. I took the vase off and set it on the window ledge. The pedestal was heavy, but I managed to lift it and take it up the stairway to the roof.

I went back to our room and awaited the chairs and pallets delivery. As I lay in bed, my mind wandered to the trial. How could I keep order among seventeen spirits with each communicating by mental telepathy? Servant and I would have to come up with some system. Also, if I was the judge, I wouldn't be the one asking questions of the witnesses or the accused. I would have to refrain from any incriminating and unwanted comments.

At 3 p.m. I heard a beep of a horn at the fence near Thorpe Lane. Looking out the window, I saw the truck from the party store pulling toward the gatehouse. I hurriedly walked down the stairs and out the door to greet the workers. There were three young men jumping out of the truck and going to the back to unload the chairs and pallets.

"They're going to the roof," I said and pointed toward the top of the gatehouse.

"This place is old," the one who appeared in charge said.

"Over five hundred years," I said.

When I led the way through the door and up the first stairs to where we would meet the spiral staircase, the workers didn't seem discouraged or reluctant to carry the chairs to the roof. It took two trips to carry the chairs and pallets. All three seemed amazed at the view from the roof.

"So, this was part of a real castle?" one of them asked.

"Yes, for several hundred years," I answered.

"You going to have a party up here?" another one asked.

"You might call it that," I said not wanting to mention my meeting with ghosts. I signed a receipt for the delivery.

"When do we pick them up?" the one in charge asked.

"Probably in two days. Maybe three. I'll ring up the shop and let you know."

With that said and done, they were off to the truck. I looked over the wall at them. They waved as they pulled back onto the street. Now, I set out to arrange the chairs and pallets.

First, I made a row of six chairs. Then I placed another row of six in front. This would be seating for the jury of twelve.

I stacked the two wooden pallets and lifted my beautiful blue upholstered chair to sit on the top of them. I would be facing the jury but about fifteen feet from them.

To my right and in front, I placed what would be the chair for King Henry. Opposite him and to my left, I set three chairs for Wolsey, Howard, and Culpeper. They would be facing Henry. Then, finally, in front of my chair and below the pallets, I put the chair for Servant. Then I counted. Twelve chairs for the jury—three chairs for the prosecutor and witnesses—a chair for King Henry—Servant's chair--and finally, my chair on the platform made of pallets above the others. I was to be the judge and had to sit in a place of authority. All was in place.

I moved back to our room and lay in the bed, my mind spinning in anticipation. Then my phone buzzed. It was a text from the clerk at the Pickled Postie. My packages had arrived. I texted back that I would step down there shortly. I looked at the time—4 p. m. I needed to get the order back to our room before Sara and the girls got back. I hurried off.

"Here they are, Mr. Cawood," the clerk said. She handed one box and two packages wrapped in plastic over the counter to me.

"I made one combined order and got three parcels," I said.

"Is that all you ordered?" she asked

"I think so. And can you reserve a table for us for breakfast in the morning. There will be four of us."

She wrote down our reservation, and I turned to leave with the three packages stacked in my arms.

"Thank you and we'll be here for breakfast."

Back at our gatehouse room, I opened the box first. It held a nice wooden gavel. Then one of the plastic wrapped packages contained my white wig. I was a bit fascinated with it. I touched it and ran my fingers through what appeared to be white hair. Then I went to the bathroom to try it on in front of the mirror. It fit really well and made me appear like some of the English judges that I had seen on television. Back in our room, I opened the package that contained the black judicial robe. I didn't try it on, but I did hold it up to me to see the length. It would be a good fit. I put them all away in an empty suitcase to hide them from the girls and Sara.

"Bobo, you should have gone with us on the boat ride," Katie said when they arrived back from their excursion to York. "We had lunch at a riverside restaurant. The boat ride was really cool."

I thought ahead to the following day. I would have a full free day before the early morning trial.

"I can go tomorrow," I said. "I would like to relax on a boat on the river."

After we walked to the Castle Inn for dinner, the sun was setting by the time we arrived back at the gatehouse. Shadows crept up the walls.

"I still think this looks like a place where you could find ghosts," Katie said. "What do you think, Bobo?"

I looked at Sara and then at what was left of Cawood Castle. "I'm sure if there are any here, they would be nice and kind."

"Oh, I don't like any ghosts," Katie said. She and Ashlynn ran in and up to their room.

We all dressed early the next morning for our appointed breakfast at the Pickled Postie. I was more relaxed thinking of our day ahead.

After breakfast we caught the 42 Bus to York and our river adventure on the boat that the girls had ridden on the day before.

Tree limbs hung over the River Ouse as the boat navigated what I thought was a rather narrow river. It wasn't like the Tennessee, Ohio, or Mississippi rivers that I had been on in America. It wasn't much wider than the creek that ran behind our house in Tennessee. However, the route provided us with a different view of York—one that I imagined the Vikings saw hundreds of years before.

For three hours, the boat plied the water with us aboard. People walked along paths near the bank on a warm May day. At the end of the ride, we decided to eat an early dinner at a riverside restaurant where Sara and the girls ate the day before.

We arrived back at the gatehouse just as it was getting dark. I looked at the time on my phone. There were just a few minutes over three hours left before I was to meet Servant on the roof. Now, I was beginning to become nervous again.

The girls went up to their room rather tired from the full day of activities. I lit the candles we had bought in York. Then I went to my suitcase where my purchases were.

"I got my gavel, wig, and robe yesterday," I told Sara. "The roof is all fixed with the chairs."

"So, you're going through with the—trial—or whatever you call it?"

"Yes. Earlier than normal. We'll begin just after midnight." I held the wig and robe up for Sara to see.

"And you're going to wear that?"

"Yes."

"Put them on. I want to take a picture to show the psychiatrist when we get home."

I closed the door to the stairway to keep the girls out. Then I took my wig and robe into the kitchen to put them on. In a couple of minutes, I was ready to step back into our room for Sara's inspection.

"Ha, ha," she laughed and covered her mouth with both hands. "You do look like an English judge. Hold still. I want a picture."

"Keep quiet. I don't want the girls to see," I said.

I took them off after the picture and waited for midnight. There would be plenty of time to slip on my wig and robe when it was time to go up and out onto the roof. We both sat on the bed. Sara listened to a book on her ear buds, and I wondered how this was going to turn out.

At fifteen minutes until midnight, I stood up and grabbed my wig and robe.

"Wish me luck," I said toward Sara.

"I wish you sanity," she responded.

I waited until I was on the roof to put the wig and robe on. There was a bit of light from the stars, but the moon had not yet reached its zenith. I went to the platform, stepped up, and sat in my blue upholstered chair. I hoped Servant would arrive before the others so we could discuss the procedures.

Just as promptly as ever, Servant appeared in front of me. He turned a complete circle and then looked back toward me.

"It appears you have everything in order," I heard him say.

"Yes. Chairs for the jurors. Three on that side for Wolsey, Howard, and Culpeper. The one on the other side for King Henry. And this one in front for you," I responded.

"Very good."

"Servant, I want to talk with you about the procedures before anyone else arrives."

"Go ahead."

"With there being seventeen spirits in total, I was concerned about all the voices through their mental telepathy. Do you have a way to silence any voices or words from all except the one who is supposed to be speaking? I don't want to hear the thoughts of any juror or witness while Henry is speaking. And I don't want to hear their thoughts while Wolsey, Catherine, or Culpeper are testifying. Can you make it where I will just hear one at a time? And no one hears anyone except the one who is supposed to be speaking?"

Servant was quiet for a minute. It appeared he was considering it.

"You didn't hear my thoughts then, did you? I can turn the reception of thoughts off. And I will do it as bailiff for all present, so that you only hear the ones who are supposed to be speaking."

"That's great," I thought.

"Now, it's time to bring in the jury," Servant said.

I looked toward the back row of six chairs. Suddenly, they were filled with six bright robes in the colors of the rainbow. There were robes of red, orange, yellow, green, blue, and indigo. Only the violet was missing.

"Here we have six archbishops," Servant began. "From your left to right are William Greenfield, William Melton, William Zouche, John Thoresby, Thomas Rotherham, and Thomas Savage. They are all free from being influenced by the witnesses or King Henry as none of them served during his reign."

"Good," I said.

"And here are the next six on the front row," Servant said as the chairs filed with six more spirits. "On your far left is Archbishop George 'Big Mountain' Montaigne in the violet robe. Next is George Neville who gave the great feast here at the castle. Then we have Archbishop John Kemp who built this gatehouse. Then in the last three chairs are the three kings who you talked to earlier—Henry III in the royal purple robe, Edward I in that red fluorescent robe, and finally Edward II in another green robe.

"There you have it. We have nine archbishops and three kings on the jury. They are all highly educated. They all know how the government should work. As you say in America, this is a jury of King Henry's peers—even though not of the same time frame."

"Thank you each for coming, I will swear you in as jurors when everyone is here," I said. "Who is next?"

The three chairs to my left suddenly filled with brightly clothed spirits.

"You remember these three," Servant said. "Here we have Cardinal Wolsey. Next to him is Thomas Culpeper. And next to Culpeper is Queen Catherine Howard."

I gazed at them. All three seemed to be looking around and then back toward the jury.

"You are here as agreed to participate in a trial of sorts of King Henry the Eighth. Thank you for coming," I said.

I saw Servant move what looked like his hand across where his mouth would have been.

"I am allowing them to speak now," he said.

"We are all glad to be here," I heard the three say in unison.

Then Servant did a similar move with his hand across his mouth. "I have now closed their mouths so that they cannot speak until spoken to."

I turned to my right and looked at the empty chair where King Henry was supposed to sit. "Is he coming?" I asked Servant.

"Are you ready?" he asked me.

I nodded my head. My heart beat rapidly. What would happen? How would King Henry react to being on trial at Cawood Castle?

It was like a bright flash when his chair filled. I was correct to get a large chair. His spirit completely filled it. I saw his head turn toward the jury and then toward the three seated across from him. His robe was a royal purple with what appeared a crown on top. Then he spoke.

"What are these three traitors doing here?" he asked and then looked directly at me. "And who are you wearing that ridiculous wig?"

I looked at Servant and motioned toward my mouth and ears. I hoped that Servant received the message that I wanted King Henry to hear me when I spoke, and I wanted to hear him when he spoke.

"I am Judge Cawood, a descendant of the Cawoods of this village. I have been chosen to preside here over your trial."

"Trial? I am King. I should not be tried. And you don't sound like an Englishman. Did I ever have any of your ancestors' heads chopped off?"

"Not that I know. I will be an impartial Judge. I live in America. The jury to your right will make any decisions. The three you list as traitors are here to testify about your actions. And Cardinal Wolsey will lead the prosecution, just as he helped you prosecute many during your reign."

"America? So, you are not an Englishman. You cannot be my judge. I was sent to America by The Great Spirit for a hundred years. If I had been king then, you traitors would not have succeeded. Your leaders would have been hanged or gone to the chopping block."

Henry then appeared to stare at Wolsey. "He is a coward and traitor. When I charged him with treason, he decided to die on the way back to London. I was going to have his head lopped off."

"Your jury is made up of nine Archbishops of York. One also served as Archbishop of Canterbury. And we also have three kings on the jury," I told Henry.

"Kings! Huh! None of those three was a Tudor. Tudors were the best royalty. And I was the greatest Tudor!"

"Nevertheless, this is the jury." I looked at Servant, my bailiff, and motioned for him to have the jury members to stand.

When they stood, I gave them an oath of office that I had made up.

"Do each of you agree to hear the case against King Henry, give it your full attention, without any preconceived notion, without any prejudice, and without fear or favor render a just verdict, so help you The Great Spirit?"

I heard them all say "Yes." Then they sat back down.

I could sense that Henry was becoming a bit riled. So, I decided to engage him in a bit of lighter conversation.

"How did you like your visit to Cawood Castle in 1541?"

His spirit appeared to move and twist. "It was a nice hunting lodge. Nothing more. Hampton Court was much more prestigious. I did get to hunt the harts and stags here. Good hunting. Good forests. I was on my Progress to the North. I brought four or five thousand with me to show these people my power. They had revolted in what they called the Pilgrimage of Grace. Unfortunately, James the Fifth of Scotland stood me up when we were supposed to meet in York. And he was my nephew.

"While I was out hunting, those two over there," he said pointing to Howard and Culpeper, "were here cavorting."

I looked down to Servant who was bowing his head.

"We have something in common, King Henry."

"What is that?"

"I was born exactly four hundred years after you died. You died on January 28, 1547, and I was born on January 28, 1947."

"A joyous occasion I am sure," he said.

"Yes. At least one was," I said and smiled.

"Perhaps both were," he said and seemed to smile. Perhaps he enjoyed a joke.

I then moved on to the business at hand.

I motioned for Cardinal Wolsey to stand up and state the charges for which the king was being tried. Servant seemed to run his hand across his mouth in the direction of Wolsey. Wolsey's spirit then stood in front of his chair.

"The charges are murder and theft. King Henry murdered two wives, including Catherine Howard who is here, Anne Boleyn, Thomas Culpeper, who is here, Thomas More, and Thomas Cromwell. And he murdered at least fifty-seven thousand others during his reign."

I looked toward Henry. I could tell he was agitated. I motioned Servant to allow Henry to respond.

"I murdered no one. Howard and Boleyn were executed for treason. They lied about their relationships with men before our marriages and their relationships with other men while we were married.

"Culpeper, over there, was one of the ones Howard was involved with. I showed mercy to him. He was to be hanged, drawn and quartered for treason. But because of my fondness for him, I showed mercy and just had his head lopped off.

"Thomas More refused to sign the oath that I was the supreme head of the Church of England. That was heresy punishable by death. He was given several opportunities to sign. He refused.

"Thomas Cromwell was found guilty of treason. He was a fine advisor after you," Henry pointed toward Wolsey, "but he was said to have done treasonous acts. He was executed according to law. I later learned that some of the charges against him were false. I regretted his legal execution.

"The fifty-seven thousand others you mention is an exaggeration. It was closer to fifty thousand. There should have been more. They were all executed legally under the law. There were traitors, horse thieves, murderers, promoters of heresy, and those who refused to recognize me as the Supreme Head of the Church of England."

King Henry then turned toward the jury. "I murdered no one. I was king. Parliament made laws—some at my suggestion. But I only enforced the laws that were in effect," he said and pointed to the three kings on the jury. "As you did during your reigns."

Wolsey then asked to speak again.

"Anne Boleyn and Catherine Howard were only guilty of adultery, if anything. You had them executed. You were guilty of adultery yourself on many occasions."

Henry stood up from his chair. I had to take control. "Henry Tudor, sit down. No one stands unless I ask them to stand." He shuffled, looked at me, and then sat down.

"I am the king," he said. "Adultery by any wife of mine is treason. I am not bound by the same rules because I was king, and I was also the Supreme Head of the Church. I can do anything. Read the law. It was never murder. It was just enforcement of the laws at that time."

I looked back toward Wolsey and motioned him to speak.

"You changed the laws on any whim. Actions that weren't against the law when they did them, you changed and made them against the law. Those are now called *ex post facto* laws."

"There was no such thing when I was king. And you, Wolsey, was a prosecutor of many or you chose the prosecutor. If I murdered anyone, you were complicit in it. But I murdered no one."

It was time to move on. "Cardinal Wolsey, would you like for either Catherine Howard or Thomas Culpeper to testify?"

"Yes," Wolsey said.

"They can do it from their chairs as soon as I swear them in," I said. I then swore both in to tell the truth, the whole truth, and nothing but the truth, so help them The Great Spirit. Catherine Howard started first.

"That fat pig murdered me," she said and pointed an accusing finger of her spirit toward Henry.

"Now, Queen Catherine," I said, "you cannot call anyone derogatory names. Just tell your story and the jury will decide the outcome."

"Yes," she said. "I apologize to the court, but I do not apologize to him." she again pointed at Henry. "I was but a child when I was betrothed to him—sixteen I believe. It was a political marriage like most of his six.

"Yes, I had boyfriends before I ever met Henry. Nobody asked me about those before I married him. For the most part, they were innocent friendships."

"For the most part?" Henry interrupted. "So, you admit to illicit relationships before you married me? All of those were supposed to be disclosed upon penalty of being found guilty of treason."

Once again, I found myself trying to keep order. "King Henry, please refrain from interrupting the witness. You can have your say when she's done." Henry sat back in his chair, but I could tell he wasn't happy with my ruling. "Go ahead Queen Catherine."

"I was barely seventeen when we married. He was forty-nine. All he wanted was some young thing to give him a son. I didn't get pregnant by him or anyone else. So, he found a way to get rid of me.

"When we left London in 1541 on our Progress to the North, I thought it would be a delightful holiday. But all he wanted to do was to hunt and show off his power. My cousin, Thomas Culpeper, was there to soothe me.

"When we were here at Cawood Castle, Henry went off hunting. I had no one to console me except for my dear cousin, Thomas. Henry accused me of things I didn't do. If Thomas and I were having relations during those four months, why did I not get pregnant? No. It was all made up. I was executed on thirteen, February, 1542, still not pregnant. I thought if I made a false confession of guilt that Henry would spare me."

I looked over at Henry and motioned that he could speak.

"You both confessed. You both were guilty of treason."

"I did love Thomas Culpeper like a brother—a beloved cousin. You weighed twenty-two stones with a belly like a barrel of ale. You couldn't get on your horse without two men helping you. Your legs had open sores that smelled to high heaven. I might say, in hindsight, death was a preferred escape from being around you," Catherine said.

Henry shook his spirit head but didn't say anything.

"Is that all you have to say, Queen Catherine?" I asked.

"Yes."

Then I looked at Wolsey. "Is Thomas Culpeper going to testify?"

Wolsey stared at Henry and then turned back to Culpeper. He nodded. "Yes, Thomas will testify."

"I don't have much to say. I was a loyal servant to Henry," Culpeper began. "I volunteered to go on the Progress to the North with about five thousand others.

"Henry always had the best places to stay for the four months we were gone. Queen Catherine was lonely. Henry was always away eating, hunting, or prancing around in his fancy clothing on the best horses."

Henry stood up and interrupted. "I did not eat that much. Just enough to nourish me. I was King so I had the best places to stay. I enjoyed hunting and riding. That is no crime. But what you did with Catherine was treason."

I held my hand up. "Henry, once again I must admonish you not to interrupt the witness. Your time will come. Sit down."

"That's about all I have to say. I was not guilty of treason," Culpeper said. "I was murdered on false allegations. I was just twenty-six years old."

I turned toward Wolsey. "Anymore testimony on the charges of murder?" I asked.

"No," Wolsey said. "We'll move on to the charges of theft."

"Theft!" Henry shouted. "I did not steal anything. I was king. All I had to do was ask for something and it was given to me. No theft—just gifts."

I motioned for Henry to sit down and be quiet. "Go ahead, Cardinal Wolsey."

"We'll start with Hampton Court, and I will testify to that theft.

"I built Hampton Court with my own money. I was very much involved with international relations—both political and religious. I wanted a nice place to entertain foreign visitors—monarchs and such. So, I built a magnificent palace—Hampton Court. I even had part of the river diverted to run through it to have running water.

"Henry came to many of the functions and parties there. Finally, he told me he wanted Hampton Court for his own. I knew the results of refusing his wishes. He would charge me with treason and forfeit all my property—including Hampton Court. So, I was forced to let him have it. It was strong-armed theft."

Henry jumped up. "See, he admits he gave it to me. Gift not theft."

I again held my hand up. "Let Wolsey finish," I said.

"That was a typical theft by Henry. If you didn't give what he wanted, he would find a way to imprison you and get what he wanted.

"But his largest theft was when he stole control of the church from the Pope and made himself the Supreme Head of the Church."

"The parliament passed that law!" Henry once again shouted. "I was king and head of the church."

I wondered if I was losing control of the trial. I looked back toward the jury. Each member appeared to be paying strict attention to the testimony.

"Henry, I don't want to hold you in contempt of court, but you must control your outbursts." He sat back in his chair and shook his head. "Go ahead Cardinal Wolsey."

"After I was gone, Henry began to close all the monasteries and take their land, jewelry, precious jewels, gold, and anything of value. He started with the small monasteries and then went on to the large.

"This was an out and out pillage and theft of everything they had. Thousands and thousands of acres of land were taken. All their earthly possessions. If any monks or priests objected, they were murdered in horrible ways—burned at the stake, hanged, drawn, and quartered, among others."

This time Henry raised his hand and looked at me. "May I speak?" he asked.

"Go ahead," I said.

"Those monks, priests, and nuns were doing horrible sinful acts. They would not recognize me as the Supreme Head of the Church.

Upon their criminal conduct being proven, their property was forfeited to the kingdom. I had wars to finance. The money from their possessions was used for that. I sold--at very reasonable prices--the land to the poor people in the area so they could farm it and graze their sheep on it. It was all for the Kingdom—for England."

Cardinal Wolsey raised his hand to be recognized to respond. "He pocketed the greatest amount of the money from what he took from the monasteries. Some went to finance a war or two, but most of it went into his private treasury."

"Any other testimony?" I asked.

"No," Wolsey answered.

I looked at the jury. "Do any of you have any questions?" I waited a full minute, but no juror asked to speak.

I turned back toward Wolsey. "Do you have a closing argument?"

"Yes."

"Go ahead."

"Henry the Eighth is a murderer and a thief."

"That's it?" I asked.

"Yes."

Then I turned to Henry. "Your closing argument?"

"I am not a murderer nor a thief," Henry said.

"That's it?" I asked again.

"Yes."

I shook my head and looked toward Servant. He was squirming in his chair. Those were the shortest closing arguments that I had ever heard in my fifty years of law practice.

"OK," I said. I looked at the jury.

"These are my instructions to you in deciding this case.

"You have listened attentively to the testimony of Cardinal Wolsey, Queen Catherine Howard, Thomas Culpeper, and King Henry.

"Now it is up to you to apply the facts and the law to the case and to what you have heard and seen. You should retire to the corner of the roof, select a jury foreman, and deliberate until you have reached a unanimous verdict. You will then tell the bailiff, Servant, that you have reached a verdict. Then the foreman will step forward and announce it in open court.

"Do you understand?"

Each of the juror spirits appeared to be nodding their heads as an affirmative response.

"You may retire to the rear where you can confer in private."

Then I looked to my left and right. "The parties and witnesses may stay seated or walk around the roof, but you must refrain from being near the jury."

Chapter Twelve

The Verdict

I looked at my phone to get the time. The whole trial, with interruptions and all, had only taken two hours. But I wasn't sure how long the jury deliberations would take. I reached into my pocket and retrieved the list of jurors in the order they were seated.

Nine Archbishops of York and three kings of England. When did they serve in their positions, and were any of them appointed by King Henry? I was hoping for a fair jury. These twelve were certainly well educated and knew the machinations of government and religion in their time.

My list of archbishops showed that all of them except for one had served many years before Henry was King. William Greenfield and William Melton were in office two hundred years before Henry was king. William Zouche and John Thoresby were a hundred and fifty years before Henry. Thomas Rotherham and Thomas Savage had lived during some of Henry's lifetime but not while he was king. George Neville and John Kemp served at least fifty years before Henry was king.

George Montaigne was the only archbishop who served after Henry's reign. He was only archbishop for four months from July 1628 until October 1628. He had been born twenty-two years after

Henry died. His brief service occurred during the reign of Charles the First whose actions would later engulf England in a civil war. He was a Stuart King. All the archbishops except for Montaigne had served when the Pope was the head of the church. Montaigne was the only archbishop on the jury who had served under the Church of England with the king as Supreme Head of the Church.

All three kings on the jury—Henry III, Edward the First, and Edward the Second—had reigned two hundred years or so before Henry the Eighth.

After I had reviewed who was on the jury, I began to wonder whether my brief instructions to them were sufficient. However, in my years of law practice I had noticed that jurors very often didn't pay attention to jury instructions. Some nodded off in slumber while they were being read. Others disregarded the instructions as they had already made up their minds. Some decided on whom they liked as witnesses or disliked as defendants. I came to the conclusion that with the type of jurors who were here, my instructions were sufficient.

I motioned Servant to join me in the far corner of the gatehouse roof. I took off my wig and unbuttoned my robe. I glanced back at the jury. The members seemed to be huddled around in a circle and discussing the case. Apparently, they were taking it seriously.

"You appeared very judgelike in your wig and robe," Servant said.

"Thanks. What do you think the jury is doing?"

"They are doing their job. They are discussing the testimony and arguments."

"Very short arguments," I said.

"Some of the jurors had their minds made up when they knew who the prosecutor and defendant were," Servant said.

"I thought that might be the case."

We looked around for the participants. Henry was leaning against the wall toward Selby staring out into the darkness. Wolsey, Catherine, and Thomas stood together toward the door to the stairway. I could see movement of their spirits as though they were a bit troubled. I looked at my phone for the time. It had only been a half hour although it seemed like longer.

"How long do you think it will take to get a verdict?" I asked Servant, knowing he would not have any inkling. Often in my practice of law, I would leave the courtroom as soon as the jury went out and waited at my office across the street. Today, as judge, I would have to wait out the process just a short distance from the jury. Fortunately, Servant had arranged it so that neither I nor the participants could hear a word of the jurors' deliberations.

"I believe we'll have a verdict before sunrise," Servant said. "Or else we may have to come back in the dark of the next midnight."

The glow of the spirits put more light on the roof of the gatehouse than the stars or moon. The sparkling robes reflected off the stone walls and floor. It was almost a hypnotizing display. Servant and I moved along the wall and very often glanced over our shoulders toward the jurors. King Henry appeared to be almost glued to the wall that faced toward Selby.

A half hour later, Servant suddenly turned. "I see movement," he said. "The jurors are heading back to their chairs."

"Oh, perhaps a verdict. I will be keen to hear it," I said. I grabbed my white judge's wig and quickly placed it on my head. I buttoned my black judicial robe and stepped toward my chair. I looked at Servant. "Approach the jury and see if they have a verdict. Also, tell King Henry, Wolsey, Catherine, and Thomas to take their seats."

Servant moved from one side to the other. The participants sat in their chairs while Servant moved toward the jury. I could see he was talking with them, but I could not hear a word that was spoken. Shortly, he turned and came toward me.

"The jury has chosen a foreman and have reached one verdict and one decision."

"One verdict? And a 'decision'?" I asked.

"Yes."

"Have the foreman to stand and make it where he can talk and listen to me."

Servant motioned toward the jury and wiped his hand across his mouth and toward his ears. Archbishop George Montaigne stood.

"If you jurors have chosen Archbishop Montaigne as your foreman, please signify by raising your right hand," I instructed. They all lifted their spirit right hands within their robes. I then moved on to find out what the jury had decided. King Henry, Wolsey, Catherine, and Thomas all appeared to be paying rapt attention.

"Tell me of your decision and verdict," I said.

Montaigne stepped forward a few feet toward me.

"Your Honor, if it pleases the Court, we have come to conclusions on the charges of murder and theft against King Henry the Eighth."

"Go ahead, please," I said.

"All of the members of the jury wanted it known how they decided and of the division within the jury. On the charge of murder, it was what you would term a hung jury, no pun intended.

"There was a vote of nine to three that Henry was guilty of murder. The nine were the archbishops who reasoned that even if he was not legally guilty, he was morally guilty. The three kings voted a 'not guilty' to the murder charge. They reasoned and said they had executed quite a few during their reigns. They said execution according to the law at the time was not murder.

"The kings further said that Catherine, Thomas, Anne Boleyn, Cromwell, and More were all tried according to the law at the time.

All confessed to treason. So, their executions were not murder but just carrying out the penalties for treason.

"As to the allegations that Henry murdered fifty thousand, or so, of other people, there was no proof offered—just the argument of Wolsey. So, in the end, the jury could not decide on the murder charges, and Henry is not convicted of those."

I looked down at Henry. He raised his right hand in triumph. When I turned my gaze toward Wolsey, Catherine, and Thomas, they appeared to be shaking their heads in disbelief.

"What about the charges of theft?" I asked.

Montaigne looked to his right, then to his left, and then back toward me.

"We do have a unanimous verdict on those charges, Your Honor."

"Please tell the court what it is."

"Guilty," Montaigne said. "All members of the jury, including the three kings, found Henry guilty of theft of the church organization from the Pope to himself. Although the theft may have benefited England in the end, it was still theft. All of the other archbishops and the three kings served and reigned when the Pope was the head of the church. Only I served as Archbishop under the Church of England. However, I agree that what Henry did was theft of the church organization. We know that parliament passed the Supremacy statute. That only makes them complicit in the theft. But they are not on trial here.

"Next, as to the charge concerning theft from the monasteries, we find him guilty. He closed the small monasteries and then the large monasteries. His purpose was to steal their precious possessions. Although some of the possessions may have been used to finance a war or two, that does not excuse the theft and the destruction of the monasteries. A very large amount of the proceeds went into his pocket.

"Lastly, as to the charge that he is guilty of theft of Hampton Court Palace from Cardinal Wolsey, we find him guilty. Henry termed it a gift. But each of us archbishops and the three kings know that when the king in power asks for something, the owner better deliver or risk losing his head on the block for treason. Wolsey built Hampton Court, and he should have been able to keep it.

"King Henry the Eighth is guilty of three counts of theft," Montaigne concluded.

Henry jumped to his feet. "I am not guilty of any theft. I took the church because we should be ruled by someone in England and not someone in Italy. The occupants of the monasteries were great sinners and treasonous. I took their property to finance England's wars. Hampton Court was a generous gift from Wolsey when we were on good terms. I am still at Hampton Court. It's a lovely place."

I looked at Montaigne and then at Henry. "King Henry, you've had your say. Please sit down until I receive further word from the jury."

Henry sat back down but waved his arms in frustration. I then looked back to Montaigne. "Did the jury make any recommendations as to what any penalty should be?"

"Yes, Your Honor, we did. After careful consideration and consultation, we decided this. King Henry the Eighth should be removed from Hampton Court and placed in the same cell at the Tower of London where Catherine Howard awaited execution and stay there permanently.

"Further, Cardinal Thomas Wolsey should possess Hampton Court Palace as the home for his spirit permanently."

I looked over toward Wolsey and Catherine. Wolsey knelt in thanksgiving. Catherine raised both arms in joy.

"I want to appeal," Henry said.

I looked down at him. "Your appeal will be to the Great Spirit. These are merely the recommendations of the jury. I, as judge, agree with their verdict, findings, and what they recommend. However, the final decision will be made by the Great Spirit. Our bailiff, Servant, will report the verdict and recommendations to the Great Spirit. In a timely fashion, I believe the Great Spirit will decide and let us all know.

"Is there anything else to take up?" I asked. Everyone was silent. "If not, I declare this trial over. Everyone may go to their place of residence for their spirits. Except, I will need to confer with my bailiff, Servant."

One by one the members of the jury appeared to lift up and float over the wall of the gatehouse toward York and some toward Scotland. Henry left last. I looked over toward Wolsey, Catherine, and Thomas. They stayed huddled in a corner. Then the spirit of Wolsey lifted and drifted off toward Leicester. I walked to Servant.

"Why are Catherine and Thomas still here?"

"They decided to stay around here with the memories of their visit in 1541 and the good times they had."

"Oh. When can you get the verdict and recommendations to the Great Spirit?"

"I am not sure. The Great Spirit is very busy. I am not sure how much effort He wants to devote to this matter. But I will go immediately and petition for an audience. It may take three hours, three days, three weeks, three months, or three years. Time is irrelevant to the Great Spirit."

"But you will let me know as soon as there is a decision?"

"Yes," Servant said.

I looked across the roof. This had certainly been an eventful early morning. Nobody would believe it.

"Servant, we have no other spirits to visit, do we?"

"No."

"We will be leaving in a few days. I hope you get a decision before then."

"I'll do my best."

"And, Servant, thank you for all your help. I hope to see you shortly"

Servant appeared to wave a hand, and he was gone.

Chapter Thirteen

Going Home

Sara was asleep when I went back down to our room. I thought she would be awake. I looked at my phone. It was 4 a.m. Only I would be awake at this hour.

I couldn't sleep and was out of bed when the sunlight blazed through the window. Coffee—I needed coffee. The happenings of the overnight hours kept running through my mind. The jury had found King Henry the Eighth guilty of theft and not guilty of murder. 'Not guilty' did not mean he was innocent—just that there was not enough evidence or law to convict him.

Then I started thinking about the recommendations of the jury. Would Henry actually lose his residence at Hampton Court and be sent to a cell in the Tower of London? Would Cardinal Wolsey be restored to Hampton Court? Would the Great Spirit impose those penalties or just ignore the trial, verdict, and recommendations? Would there be any outcome of the trial? Did Servant and I put on the trial, bring in the Archbishops of York, three kings, Wolsey, Catherine, and Culpeper for nothing? The decision wasn't in my hands. At least Catherine and Culpeper decided to stay around the area.

Sara joined me at the table. "So, how did the trial go? Did King Henry the Eighth show up?"

"Yes. Everybody was there."

"I see your judge's wig and robe over there on the floor. Were you the judge?"

"Yes."

"What was the verdict?"

"Not guilty of murder, but guilty of theft."

"What? Murder is very serious but theft? Seems like a not very serious charge."

"Well, he wasn't going to be executed for murder since he is already dead. The theft charges were serious. He stole the governance of the church from Rome. He stole all the property of the monasteries. He stole Hampton Court from Cardinal Wolsey."

"But they can't recover that from him, can they?"

"Only concerning Hampton Court. The jury recommended that Henry's spirit be banished to a cell in the Tower of London, and Cardinal Wolsey's spirit be restored to Hampton Court."

"Recommended? Who decides?"

"The Great Spirit."

"God?"

"Yes."

"When?"

"I don't know. Servant is going to present the jury's findings to the Great Spirit when he's allowed," I said.

"So, you don't know a time," Sara said and glanced out the window. "Who are you going to talk with tonight?"

"Nobody. It' over. No more spirits to visit. We're going home at the end of the week."

"That's the best news that I've heard lately. Three days. And remember you promised to see a psychiatrist when we get home."

"Yes."

Sara and the granddaughters found things to do in York and Selby over the next three days. I went with them two days. One day I stayed at the gatehouse and waited for the party store employees to come and fetch the chairs from the roof.

"How did your roof-top party go?" one of the young men from the party store asked. "Looks like you had twelve chairs lined up and the others just left and right. Did you have a chorus singing?"

"No. It was just the way we were sitting. The 'party' went fine."

There was no word from Servant over the three days. I waited, but he did not appear. I began to think that maybe Sara was correct. Perhaps I was dreaming or having some visions or hallucinations. I busied myself with packing, walking around the roof top, and going each day to the Pickled Postie. I was going to miss the village, the Jolly Sailor, the Ferry Inn, All Saints Church, and the Castle Inn. My walks in the Garth behind the gatehouse seemed to soothe my own spirit. If the visits were all a part of my imagination, they were well perceived in my mind.

On the day we were to leave, I walked early to the Pickled Postie. Our new friend, John, stood at the counter.

"Chris, what's up for today?"

"Getting ready to leave. Going home to Tennessee. Catching the 42 to Selby and the train from there to London."

"Let me take you. I have a friend who can help. We'll get all four of you in our cars and put your suitcases in the boots. We can carry you directly to the train depot."

I looked at my phone for the time. "In an hour. Will that do?"

"Yes."

I thanked the young lady at the counter for all her courtesies during our stay and walked back to the gatehouse. I was met by our granddaughters.

"We're going home!" Katie shouted. "I want to thank you, Bobo, for finding this wonderful place for us. At first, I was afraid there would be ghosts here. But we never saw a single ghost. Ashlynn and I would wake up every night to check. But no ghosts. I would stay here again."

I nodded my head. No ghosts for them. All the spirits for me.

"Bring your suitcases down. It's time to go to the train. John is going to pick us up."

I looked back at the gatehouse as we loaded our suitcases in John's and his friend's cars. This would probably be my last time to see it. All those who had gone before and came to visit me probably felt the same way.

We passed the Castle Inn, parts of Selby, and the Selby Abbey on our ride to the train. We were just a half hour early for our departure. Handshakes and hugs with our new friend were also sad. I looked around to see if Servant had followed. No sign of him. Had the Great Spirit made a decision? I would probably never know. At least my judge's wig and robe were safely packed away to remind me of all that I had experienced here.

It was a two-hour train ride to London. Then we caught the tube for an hour's journey from King's Cross to Heathrow. The plane was on time. We left in the dark but caught up to a glorious sunset out my window within two hours. Then I went to sleep.

A week later I sat in a friendly psychiatrist's conference room in Knoxville, Tennessee, as I had promised Sara. He had a Greek name that I could barely pronounce, so I just called him Dr. K.

I had seen no spirits or ghosts since the day of the trial. Even Servant had deserted me. But that was why I was here—to discuss my seeing ghosts or spirits. Dr. K had given me several tests. They were all on an electronic tablet. I took the Rorschach test that psychologists use to examine personality characteristics and emotional functioning. Then there was a memory test, a math test, and an English grammar test. I wasn't sure why these tests were necessary.

"So, you say your wife wanted you to come in for a visit because you were seeing ghosts on a recent trip to England?" he asked.

"Yes, I prefer to call them spirits."

"Your tests are all within normal ranges. Even your memory test is good for a man of your age. Now, tell me about seeing these spirits."

"Over a period of a week or so, I was visited by seventeen or so spirits of people who had lived or visited the castle gatehouse where we were staying."

"Hm. Could you see them and talk to them? Did they all come at one time?"

"Only once did they come at one time—three days before we left. Yes, I could see them and talk to them."

"Did they talk to you?"

"Yes, in a strange way."

"How's that?"

"By mental telepathy. I would think a question and they would hear it. They would respond in the same way."

"So, no actual sound waves? Interesting. Did your wife or anyone else see these spirits or hear them?"

"No. They told me that only the one they appointed could see and hear them."

"When was the first time?"

"Early morning of the next day after we arrived. The first one was named Servant. He said he had lived there in the 1400s and 1500s. He was my source to bring the others."

"Any famous spirits?"

"Probably the ones that most people would be acquainted with were King Henry the Eighth and Cardinal Wolsey. There were other kings of England and Archbishops of York. What they had in common was that they had lived at the castle or, at least, visited."

Dr. K smiled. "How did Henry the Eighth and Cardinal Wolsey get along?"

"Not well. We had a trial on the last night. Archbishops and other kings were on the jury. Wolsey was the prosecutor. Henry was charged with murder and theft."

"Oh, I see. He did kill a lot of people—two wives as I recall."

"Yes. One of the wives, Catherine Howard, was a witness."

"What was the outcome of the trial?"

"Not guilty of murder because of the law at the time but guilty of theft. He stole the church, closed the monasteries, took their possessions, and stole Hampton Court from Wolsey."

"What did you do to him?"

"Nothing. We just reported it to the Great Spirit to make a decision."

"The 'Great Spirit.' Is that the same as God?"

"Yes. I believe," I said. Then I saw Dr. K making notes on his pad.

"Do you believe in God?" he asked.

"Yes."

"Spirits and souls are all involved in the Christian religion. Are you a Christian?"

"Yes."

"I have counseled with others who have reported seeing and talking with spirits of departed relatives. I don't make judgments on whether they have or not. I don't know. Yours are different since they weren't departed relatives."

"Well, two of them were ancestors of mine. One was from the 1200s and the other from the 1300s."

"I see. Many Christians believe that when the physical body dies, the soul or spirit returns to God—maybe to Heaven. But what you're telling me is that these spirits hung around the earth."

"Exactly. They wouldn't take up much room—if any."

"If that is so, there would be billions of spirits all over the world. Maybe that's what I read in the Bible in Hebrews that 'we are surrounded by a great cloud of witnesses.'"

"Yes, but Servant told me the spirits could do nothing of a physical nature. They couldn't open doors or turn knobs. He said if they could do that, it would be total chaos on the earth. They just hover or go hither and yon until the final day."

"Interesting. Now, when you were in England, you had researched much about all these spirits that you saw? Is that correct? You may have had visions or dreams about them since your mind had dwelt on them for some time."

"All except Servant who was the first one I encountered. I didn't know he existed."

"Ok. Have you seen any since you returned home?"

"No."

"I don't think you have any psychiatric problems. All of your tests are good. Whether you saw and spoke with spirits, I cannot judge. I don't think there's any need for follow-up meetings. Wait here. I'll be back in a few minutes. I need to make a few entries on my records and take a phone call."

The door closed. I grasped my hands together. I wasn't crazy. He didn't think there was anything wrong with my mind. Others had seen and talked with spirits. I wasn't alone.

Just then across the room in another chair there was a golden sparkling vision. When it settled, I could see that it was Servant. Before I realized it, I shouted, "Servant. How did you get here?"

Then I remembered that we communicated by mental telepathy and raised a hand to close my mouth.

"By train, plane, and automobile," I heard him say. "No, really the Great Spirit placed me here. Remember how He sent King Henry the Eighth to America from 1690 to 1790 to observe the American revolution? He can take care of travel for us."

"Yes, I remember you telling me that. But it's been ten days. I thought you had deserted me."

"Time is of little consequence to the Great Spirit or me."

I looked at the door to be sure Dr. K wasn't coming. Then I crouched lower toward Servant. "Did you get the verdict of the jury to the Great Spirit?"

"Yes."

"Did He respond? Don't keep me waiting."

Spirit appeared to rub his chin as though he was enjoying keeping me waiting. "Well," he said.

"Go on," I almost shouted.

"He accepted the jury's verdict and recommendations."

"So, what has happened?"

"King Henry the Eighth is now enjoying a lovely cell at the Tower of London."

"And Cardinal Wolsey and Hampton Court?"

"He is back there to the palace he built. And loving it."

"Anything else?" I asked.

"Catherine Howard and Thomas Culpeper were allowed to stay in the Village of Cawood. You might see them if you go back."

Just then Dr. K came back into the room. He saw that I was crouched in my chair and smiling.

"Is everything OK?" he asked.

"Yes. Wonderful," I answered.

"You're free to go then. Thank you for coming in."

"Yes." I looked toward where Servant had been. He was still there. But then he waved and disappeared through the window.

THE END

Acknowledgments

Thanks to all the kind people of London, Selby, York and the village of Cawood for showing me around and giving me vital information.

A special thanks to John Cattanach who lives across the street from the Cawood Castle Gatehouse and provided needed transportation and input on my book.

Also by Chris Cawood

A partial list of books by Chris Cawood available for purchase on Amazon:

Tennessee's Coal Creek War – set in 1890s in East Tennessee

My Aunt's Closet – A novel set in Tennessee

The Spring of '68 – A love story novel going back to the events of 1968

Murder on Route 66 – A murder mystery set on the famous Route 66 of Oklahoma, New Mexico, and Arizona

Printed in Great Britain
by Amazon

30173096R00092